JIMMY CONNORS
HOW TO PLAY
TOUGHER TENNIS

JIMMY CONNORS
HOW TO PLAY TOUGHER TENNIS

Simple strokes and "streetfighter" instincts. They're the keys to Jimmy Connors' success on the pro tennis tour. Now, he helps you find your own formula for success!

A
tennis
MAGAZINE
BOOK

BY JIMMY CONNORS WITH ROBERT J. LaMARCHE

Published by Golf Digest/Tennis, Inc.
A New York Times Company
5520 Park Avenue
Box 395
Trumbull, Connecticut 06611-0395

Trade book distribution by
Simon and Schuster
A division of Simon & Schuster, Inc.
Simon & Schuster Building
Rockefeller Center
1230 Avenue of the Americas
New York, New York 10020

First printing
Manufactured in the
United States of America
Cover and book design by Michael Brent
Printing and binding by
R. R. Donnelley & Sons, Company

Library of Congress Cataloging-in-Publications Data
Connors, Jimmy, 1952–
    Jimmy Connors, how to play tougher tennis.
    "A Tennis magazine book."
    1. Tennis.   I. LaMarche, Robert J.   II. Title.
III. Title: How to play tougher tennis.
GV990.C66   1986   796.342   85-72331
ISBN 0-914178-78-4

Acknowledgments
Special thanks to the Sonesta Sanibel
Harbour Resort in Ft. Myers, Fla., for
the use of its tennis facilities in filming
photo sequences. The authors also
express their gratitude to Lorne
Kuhle, David Schneider and Tim
Wilkison for their assistance in photo
sessions.

Photo Credits
All photos taken by Stephen Szurlej/TENNIS
magazine with the following exceptions:
Michael Brent—20, 88, 101, 178
Todd Friedman—185
Fred Mullane—16, 72, 73, 86, 96, 124
Carol Newsom—33
R & A Photo Features—49

Cover photo by Richard Walters

CONTENTS

102

ADVANCED STROKES & STRATEGIES

102

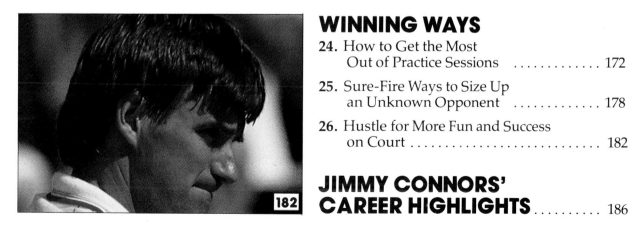

182

WINNING WAYS

JIMMY CONNORS' CAREER HIGHLIGHTS

INTRODUCTION

I got my first close-up and in-person look at Jimmy Connors through a telephoto lens in 1976 at the U.S. Clay Court Championships in Indianapolis, Indiana. A reporter for The Indianapolis Star, I had managed to wrangle a photographer's tournament credential from the newspaper's sports department and planted myself on the stadium court sideline to take some action photos.

The player I focused on was dynamic. He threw his entire body into his shots. He grunted, he fought, he laughed, he argued. But most impressive of all was the way he hustled for every ball. His determination and tenacity were extraordinary. Compressed into my viewfinder was an image of pure energy, a force which to that point in Connors' career had already helped him capture 49 singles titles.

Today, with 105 titles to his credit, including two Wimbledon and five U.S. Open crowns, Connors remains a vibrant force in tennis. His trademark is still the aggressive, powerful, hustling game that in large measure helped fuel the sport's explosion in popularity during the early 1970's.

And while he may have lost a step in speed and mellowed somewhat over the last few years, he has more than made up for it with experience. After all, you don't stay ranked among the top four players in the world for

Court hustler: Connors' aggressive, powerful game (left) helped fuel the sport's explosion in popularity.

A gripping assignment: Szurlej (on ladder) gets an aerial shot of a Connors grip (center) while LaMarche looks on.

more than 12 years, as he has, unless you're willing to learn from past matches and add new dimensions to your game. Connors became a smarter player.

That tremendous wealth of tennis knowledge and experience is the focus of *How to Play Tougher Tennis.* Over the course of two and a half years, Connors, who serves as the World Playing Editor for TENNIS magazine, met with me for intensive interviews numerous times to lay the groundwork for his first tennis instruction book.

Those interviews and subsequent discussions formed the basis for articles which have appeared, or will appear, in future issues of TENNIS under Connors' byline. They have been carefully edited and arranged to create *How to Play Tougher Tennis.*

On the following pages, you'll find a unique blend of the superstar's insights into the game's strokes and strategies, as well as full-color sequence and tournament-action photos. All have been designed to help you improve and get more enjoyment from playing tennis.

As Connors told me at the start of the project, "I don't want the people who read this book to go out on court and feel they have to work like mad to win matches. I want them to play better tennis, but to enjoy the game and its many benefits as well. Above all, I want them to have fun."

That's what *How to Play Tougher Tennis* is all about. Enjoy.

—Robert J. LaMarche
Senior Editor
TENNIS *magazine*

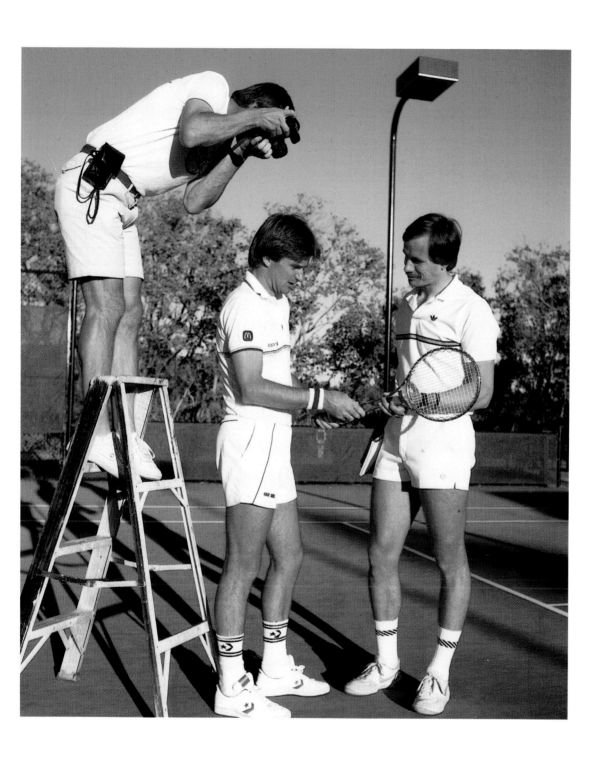

HOW TO KEEP THE GAME IN PERSPECTIVE

I don't think that too many people today can honestly say that they really enjoy their jobs. I guess I'm one of the lucky ones because tennis has always been much more than a profession for me. It's been a way of life, a happy way of life.

The game has brought me more money and fame than I ever dreamed was possible when I was a young boy growing up in Illinois. It has provided me with lots of exercise through the years. It has given me an education in terms of traveling to nearly every corner of the world and meeting new and fascinating people. It has helped me develop my inner confidence and determination to a high level. But, perhaps most importantly, tennis has been a lot of fun.

That's the bottom line in the game for me. If it weren't for that element of fun, I probably would have burned out on tennis a long, long time ago. I believe that any player—whether a beginner or a seasoned pro—must enjoy playing the game in order to reach his or her full potential.

I've always thought that the players who get a kick out of being on court, who enjoy throwing themselves 100 percent into every match, are the most dangerous. They're the toughest opponents to beat. And that's the type of toughness I'd like you to develop in your game by reading this book. I know from watching a lot of players in my career that when the sport ceases to be enjoyable and becomes an obsession, attitude and performance on court seem to self-destruct.

So it's important for you to keep the game in perspective, regardless of your ability. How did I do it? The answer is simple: By enjoying myself on the court as I grew up.

For as long as I can remember, tennis has been an important part of my life. Even before I was born, I guess you could say that the path to my career in the game was already being prepared. As the story goes, my mom, while she was still pregnant with me, walked up the street to a construction site in our neighborhood and asked the builders to stop by our house to grade our backyard for a tennis court. They eventually did and that court became my early training ground.

The court was a central hub of activity around our house because my mom and grandma were good players and fine teaching pros. So the opportunity was always at my fingertips for me to get into tennis. However, I never felt forced to become a tennis player.

I certainly had a lot of other interests to choose from. They ranged from riding horses, mini-bikes and go-carts to playing the traditional team

More than a profession: Tennis has been a way of life for me, a happy way of life.

sports that can be found in any neighborhood in the U.S. In fact, we had the perfect setup for baseball and football because there was a huge field in front of our house and about 20 to 30 kids lived within walking distance. After school each day, that field was crawling with future athletes.

But it wasn't until I was on an organized football team in eighth grade that I decided to hang up my cleats forever. My football career lasted exactly one play—the first play of the first game of the first season I played. I was small but I could run well, so they put me in the backfield. I took the first handoff and was immediately leveled by a kid who must have weighed 180 pounds. I woke up an hour later a little bit groggy, but clear-headed enough to make the choice to shed the shoulder pads.

Still, I didn't commit myself to a career in tennis until I was 16 or 17. Today, juniors seem to be making that important decision at 13 or 14. Heck, at that age, I didn't know what I wanted to do the next day, let alone for the next 15 years, and I don't think kids have changed that much.

What has changed is the big money that's now available in the game. It tends to turn the heads of youngsters, parents and coaches away from the competitive, fun aspects of tennis. As a result, the sport becomes a business which creates incredible pressure.

That's tragic for many kids because they're worn out by the time they realize they can't make it into the big leagues. At that point, the pressure to succeed in tennis has left such a sour taste in their mouths that they turn away from the game entirely.

Fortunately, I never had to confront that situation. After my rude awakening to the harsh reality of life on the football field, I began to appreciate more fully the advantages of playing tennis over team sports— besides the reduced likelihood of serious injuries. The first and most obvious advantage is that you don't have to go out and find nine or 10 guys to play with you. All you need is one player. You can play at your own pace, too, whether it's an hour of social tennis or three tough sets.

Tennis with a smile: Whether I'm at Wimbledon (far left) or a smaller event (left), I enjoy myself. I'm not afraid to smile.

There also isn't any scarcity of players to hit with. If you want to work on your game, you can usually find a slightly more advanced player who will stretch you to your limits and help you improve. Or if you're a C player who just wants to get a half-hour of exercise out in the fresh air, it's easy to find someone who plays at your level and shares the same objective.

Then there's the advantage of being able to develop your inner confidence by playing tennis. On the tennis court, you're on your own. You have to make quick decisions and deal with pressure all the time. That kind of experience is going to help you in every aspect of your life.

Finally, tennis doesn't know any age limitations. It's been promoted as a sport for a lifetime and I don't know anyone who can argue with that slogan. A trip to any local tennis club is practically guaranteed to include sights of 70- and 80-year-olds smiling proudly after hitting winners, as well as young boys and girls bursting with seemingly endless energy.

What's more, as you age as a tennis player, you gain valuable experience. So it's not uncommon for older, "over-the-hill" veterans to beat young hot shots because they are usually wiser on court. They've been around longer, earning their stripes, so to speak, and they know how to get the job done in specific playing situations.

Clearly, tennis is a game of interesting, unending challenges. And in my book, that's what makes the sport so much fun. Sure, you can adopt a more serious, businesslike attitude toward the game and it may work for a while. But you won't stay at the top for long because you won't be enjoying yourself.

I'm proud of my 100-plus pro titles and they look great in the record-book, but all of them take a back seat in importance to the fact that I had a hell of a good time earning them. That's why I think the best tennis advice I can ever give you is to keep the game fun. Don't become so intense on court that you're afraid to smile or laugh. I guarantee you'll see your game improve almost instantly. You'll be a tougher player.

No holds barred: Selecting a grip is a matter of personal preference. I use a Continental grip.

GRIPPING THE RACQUET:
FIND WHAT WORKS BEST FOR YOU

I t might surprise you to hear me say this, but after all my years in the game, I don't know what kind of grip I use to hit the ball. In fact, I'll bet a lot of the pros couldn't tell you the technical names for their grips. What counts is that we all feel comfortable with them and can find them in a split second during a point without having to think about making a switch.

I'm probably different from many of my fellow pros, though, because I use only one grip for every stroke I own. Whether I'm hitting a forehand, a volley, an overhead, a lob, a slice serve or a kick serve, I've got just one grip. It's the same even on my two-handed backhand (see photo below), except that my right hand is on the handle, too.

I've been using my old, reliable grip for as long as I can remember, and that's going back a long way. I found it by simply picking up the racquet and gripping the handle the way it felt most comfortable in my hands.

I think that's the best way for you to find your grip, too. I don't believe that instructors should force-feed students a specific grip or two for every shot. Finding out which grip is most comfortable for you and what it's effect will be on your strokes and style of play requires some experimentation. Your final choice should be a matter of personal preference.

If I had to classify my grip, I suppose it would be the Continental type (below). This grip is very basic and versatile because with it, you don't have to change grips often. You can use it to hit forehands, backhands, volleys and serves. I also think it's a good grip to start with because it can be

Two-Handed Backhand Grip

Continental Grip

I *don't believe that instructors should force-feed students a specific grip or two for every shot.*

used as a reference point to help you find other common grips.

To hold your racquet with a Continental grip, place the long, angled part of your palm (see opposite page) flat against the back side of the handle. Now, grip the racquet and spread your index finger slightly as if you were ready to pull the trigger of a gun. Your hand should end up in a position similar to the one shown on the previous page.

From this grip, a simple turn of the hand one way or the other in varying degrees will produce the other most commonly taught grips. For example, a slight turn to the right if you're a right-hander, or left if you're a lefty like me, and you'll have an Eastern forehand grip (below left) that's good for control and producing moderate amounts of topspin.

Turn your hand farther in the same direction and the palm of your hand will support the bottom of your handle more than the back side. These types of grips are called semi-Western or Western forehand grips (below) and are best used to produce heavy topspin shots. One of their disadvantages is that they put your hand so far to one side of the handle, you might find it hard to make a quick switch to a backhand grip.

To find good backhand grip, go back to the Continental starting grip and turn your hand in the opposite direction. By turning your hand slightly as you did for the forehand grips, you'll arrive at an Eastern backhand grip (below, far right).

Remember, choose grips that are comfortable for you. Then, practice them until you can switch grips quickly without thinking. A great place to do that is off the court when you're listening to the radio, watching television or just talking with friends. That way, you'll be able to concentrate better on making solid contact with the ball.

Eastern Forehand Grip

Semi-Western Forehand Grip

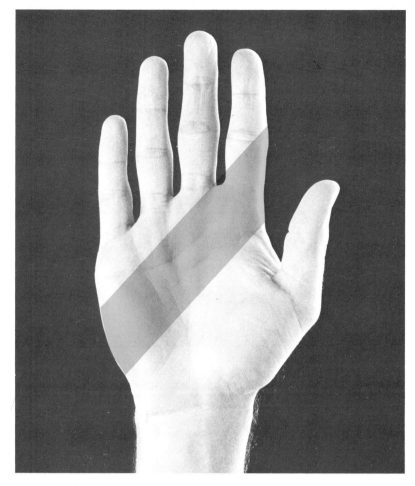

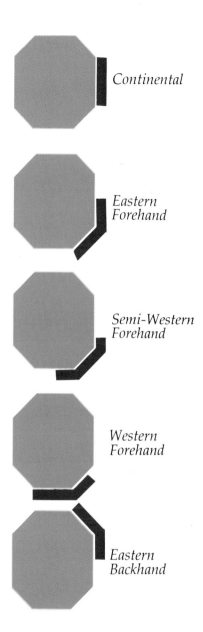

Continental

Eastern
Forehand

Semi-Western
Forehand

Western
Forehand

Eastern
Backhand

FINDING A GRIP

The key to finding grips is to first locate the meaty, diagonal part of your hand's palm shown above. Then, simply place this area on your racquet handle according to the end-view grip illustrations on the right.

Because I'm left-handed, all of the photos on the bottoms of these pages show grips from a lefty's perspective. To be fair, the illustrations here were drawn for right-handers. If you're a lefty like me, simply reverse the hand positions on the end-view grip diagrams.

Western Forehand Grip

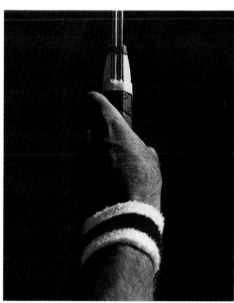

Eastern Backhand Grip

THE GROUND STROKES: KEEP THEM SIMPLE

Although I'm a baseliner, I always feel as if I should attack, as if I should do something to force the action and, at the same time, give people what they want to see. That attitude has probably cost me a few matches over the years, but it's the way I enjoy playing. I'll never change.

I think the key to my ground strokes is simplicity. For forehands and backhands, I get ready early, I take the racquet straight back, I make contact with the ball out in front of me using a fairly level stroke, and I take a full follow-through. There's nothing complex about my swing and no excess motion that could make timing the hit difficult.

That's the way I was taught to play tennis as a kid and I haven't changed my strokes at all through the years. They've always been a perfect match for my aggressive game—compact strokes that can produce power.

What really helped me develop such simple ground strokes were the courts where I learned to play. They were very fast and the bounce was always low, so I had to get a good jump on the ball. I couldn't afford to waste much time on what seemed to be unnecessary racquet movement and the answer was a short, straight backswing, which was taught to me by my mother and grandmother. It made it much easier for me to time my ground strokes, too.

Of course, some tennis experts have criticized my ground strokes throughout my career, saying I don't have much margin for error over the net with them. But because they've been a part of my game for so long, I've learned to adjust on court so that they stay consistent.

In fact, I feel as comfortable now with my game and my ground strokes as I ever have. I know what I can do with my game, and that lets me really go for my shots with confidence.

On the following pages, with the help of sequence photos, I'll show you my ground strokes and describe what I think are their keys. If you don't feel you're hitting your ground strokes as well as you should, think about my key points. Maybe they'll help put you on a winning track.

Power generator: The source of my power on backhands is a full upper-body turn (left) that lets me explode into the ball quickly and efficiently.

KEYS TO THE GROUND STROKES

THE FOREHAND

PIVOT YOUR UPPER BODY

I'm prepared for my forehand and backhand ground strokes very early, as you can see in the photo sequences here. My eyes, reflexes and ability to anticipate shots all work together to help me get a quick jump on my opponent's returns.

I've played tennis so long, it's almost instinctive now, but as soon as I see the ball come off the strings of the racquet across the net, I begin turning my shoulders sideways (see photos 1). This upper-body turn does two things. First, it starts my racquet back quickly. And second, it coils my body (2 and 3) so I can really explode into the ball on my shots.

THE BACKHAND

TAKE YOUR RACQUET BACK IN A SIMPLE MOTION

Players use different stroking styles to suit their games. For example, I like a simple, compact swing that has no excess motion to throw off my timing.

That's obvious when you take a look at photos 4 and 5 of my backswings on both sides. I just bring the racquet straight back. It's one of the reasons why I've been so consistent through the years despite my aggressive game. A simple backswing also lets me disguise my shots. I can pound the ball, come over it a little or slice it off the same backswing.

MEET THE BALL SOLIDLY OUT IN FRONT

Once my racquet's back, then I feel I'm prepared for anything they throw at me—fast or slow, high or low. My forward stroke is as simple as my backswing: It's pretty flat and I always try to meet the ball out in front (6).

The source of my power on ground strokes comes from two things: leaning into the ball and uncoiling my body by opening my hips and shoulders (7) during the stroke.

FOLLOW THROUGH COMPLETELY

I let the weight of my racquet head do a lot of work for me when I hit a ground stroke. It helps me power through the ball at impact and into a natural follow-through out in front, as you can see in photos 8 and 9 on the left.

I think of the follow-through as a director of my forehand and backhand. It helps guide the direction of my shots. And as I'm finishing a shot, I'm already starting to get back into position for the next shot. You can't just stand there and admire your shot; it's history. You have to stay on your toes and be prepared to move quickly so you can keep the pressure on.

The final ingredient: A full follow-through (right) improves pace and placement.

UNDERSTANDING THE FUNDAMENTALS OF SPIN

Even if you hit relatively flat ground strokes like I do, it's very important that you understand the basics of putting spin on the ball.

Why? First, that knowledge will enable you to use spin shots whenever the occasion calls for them. Second, and perhaps just as important, it will help you recognize the type of spin your opponent is going to put on the ball by watching his swing. Never underestimate the value of that advantage because it can be a key factor in preparing for your return.

There are two basic types of spin that can be put on a ball with different strokes: topspin and underspin, or slice. A third, sidespin, is also used occasionally, but I'll talk more about that in Chapter 20.

Topspin has been used in the game for a long, long time, but it wasn't until the mid-1970's that it really caught hold. Sweden's Bjorn Borg and Argentina's Guillermo Vilas were the two players who were most responsible for the big boom in the use of topspin. Their success at the pro level prompted even club level players to add it to their games.

In order to impart topspin to a ball, you've got to swing your racquet forward along a low-to-high path, meeting the ball with your racquet face vertical. This type of stroke creates an upward brushing effect that makes the ball spin up and away from you.

There are three advantages to using topspin (see illustration A). First, a shot hit with topspin will clear the net higher so it gives you a better margin for error. Second, the spin makes the ball dip down into the court quickly so fewer topspin shots will sail long.

Finally, a topspin shot

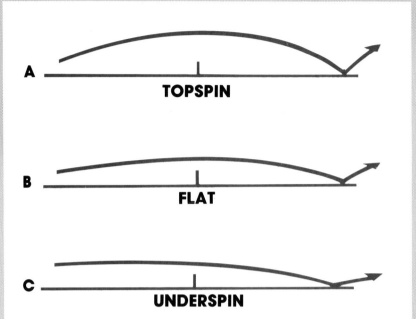

The effects of spin: A ball hit with topspin (see illustration A above) has a high clearance over the net, dips into the court quickly and kicks high toward the backcourt. A shot hit with little spin has a lower arc (B) and bounces normally. An underspin ball travels more slowly through the air and usually skids low off the court surface (C).

bounces higher off the court than a flat ground stroke (see illustration B) and kicks toward the backcourt. If a player isn't expecting a topspin shot, he can get forced deep behind his baseline or get caught flat-footed and have to make a return from around head or shoulder level. Having faced Borg and Vilas so many times in my career, I can tell you that you'd be wise to avoid both situations and take the ball on the rise after it bounces.

Underspin, or slice, is just the opposite of topspin. It's produced by hitting the ball with a high-to-low swing. The ball will spin back toward you as it leaves your racquet face and flies across the net.

The advantages to underspin are that you don't have to hit the ball hard to make it go deep and that the ball tends to bounce lower than a flat ground stroke. In fact, it skids off the court surface (see

illustration C) and forces an opponent to bend low for his return and hit the ball high enough to clear the net. For that reason, an underspin ball is used quite often by players on approach shots. The return's slower speed and low bounce enables them to move closer to the net and perhaps pick off a rising shot from an opponent.

So remember, if you want to hit with topspin, brush the back of the ball with a low-to-high forward swing. If you want to produce underspin, brush under the ball with a high-to-low stroke.

In order to anticipate what type of spin your opponent is about to use, look for a low backswing to indicate topspin and a high backswing for underspin. For advice on how to handle both types of bounces, high and low, see Chapter 9.

STROKING MECHANICS:
TOPSPIN & UNDERSPIN GROUND STROKES

TOPSPIN BASICS

To hit with topspin, take your racquet back below the level at which you plan to make contact with the ball (above).

From that low starting point, swing forward along a gradual upward path and meet the ball with a vertical racquet face.

A high follow-through will serve as confirmation that you've swung from low to high and brushed upward on the ball.

UNDERSPIN BASICS

A high backswing above the level where you're going to meet the ball is the first step in imparting underspin or slice.

Your forward stroke should be from high to low. At the point of contact, try to keep your racquet face vertical.

Complete your underspin stroke with a full follow-through out in front of your body. Don't cut your swing short.

THE SERVE:
STRIVE FOR CONSISTENCY

You won't find my name on any list of pros who own big, explosive first serves. But each time I step up to the baseline, I've got the ball in my hand and nobody can play until I make the first move.

I'm in absolute control. And when I make my delivery, I know I'm not going to overpower players very often. I'll serve to certain spots and change pace to keep receivers guessing.

I've learned that at the pro level today, it really doesn't matter how big you serve. The bottom line, as I see it, is being able to set up your second shot with your serve. That's the key.

It's obvious from what I've just said that I believe consistency is a greater serving strength than raw power. About the only drawback to developing such a level of consistency is that it can make you complacent or reluctant to try new ways to punch up your serve. I know because I've been there.

When I was growing up, I didn't have the height or strength to hit flat, powerful serves. So I just started releasing the ball more behind my head on the service toss to help me spin the ball into play and start off the point. I used basically the same serve until the Queens event before Wimbledon in 1982 because it never got me into trouble and I had the solid ground game to back it up.

But as I got older, I realized I could use a few more free points off my serve each match. To be able to hit an unreturnable serve or even an ace now and then became more important.

The change I eventually made was a very small one—I simply tossed the ball farther out in front and to the side of my body (see the photo sequence that follows). But it paid off in a big way. Although I had

A solid weapon: My flat serve creates situations where I can pounce on balls and make things happen early in a point.

It really doesn't matter how big you serve. The bottom line is being able to set up your second shot with your serve.

been using the new flat serve in practice for some time, I didn't have the guts to try it in an actual match situation until Queens in 1982. You know, old habits are hard to break. I thought, "Well, if there's any time to do it, it's now on grass where my chances of getting some easy points are better."

The serve worked. I won the title at Queens and, two weeks later, the Wimbledon crown. The new toss allowed me to put more of my body weight into my serves, while reducing pressure on my back. It also forced me to take a step farther into the court, which made it possible for me to play a little more serve-and-volley tennis.

In short, my modified toss made me even more aggressive on court. Before improving the serve, I was like a tiger lurking on the baseline in a match, slugging things out and looking for the eventual short ball that would allow me to attack. Now, I'm not lurking so much. My flat serve is creating situations where I can pounce on balls and make things happen earlier than before.

Sure, my serve still doesn't rank near the top of the list of hard servers in the game. But I can use more variety now when starting points and, at the same time, enjoy the payoff that my serving consistency provides. I'm winning free points off it every so often and I'm getting a high percentage of first serves in play, so my opponents can't take advantage of it very often. My flatter serve has made me more of a threat on court.

The following pages feature a high-speed photo sequence of my service motion, along with my comments on some of the technical keys I feel are important in any serve.

My advice to you is simple: Strive for consistency on your serves, but always keep looking for ways to improve. Start with a basic flat serve and build on that weapon.

Taking the offensive: A good service toss forces you to step into the court (left) and attack the return.

KEYS TO THE FLAT SERVE

RELAX TO START YOUR SERVICE MOTION

Before I worked up the nerve to try my new ball toss during an actual match, my serve was just a means of throwing the ball in there and starting the point off. I couldn't really use it as the weapon it should be.

Now, though, I make sure I have a specific target in mind as I start my motion (photo 1 below). Then, I begin the serve by rocking my weight off my front foot and onto my back foot (2). From this point on, all of my body movement will be forward, into the court.

As I bring up my racquet behind me, I lift my right arm and release the ball in a smooth, relaxed motion.

This is the point where, under match conditions in the past, I'd usually revert to using my old, over-the-head ball toss. I complete my new toss by allowing my tossing arm to continue to move upward smoothly, well after the ball has left my hand (3). That helps to keep my shoulders turned sideways to the net and to lift the ball accurately.

Notice that the ball is rising out in front of my body. In fact, it's inside the baseline, too.

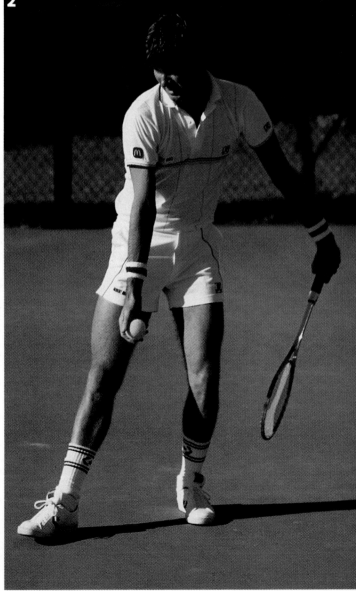

3

COIL AND UNCOIL YOUR BODY AS YOU SWING

In my career, I've heard a lot of good servers say that one of the basic keys to serving is being able to coil and uncoil your body like a spring. I think the analogy's a good one.

The coiling action starts with your shoulder turn and ends when you cock your racquet behind you (4). At this point in my motion, my body weight is shifting onto my front foot.

The uncoiling action starts as soon as you start your racquet up to make contact, as I'm doing in photo 5. My shoulders are still sideways to the net, but they'll pivot as I get near the contact point and add some punch to the serve.

I think the legs—and how they work to help you push off the court and into the ball (6)—are an often-overlooked part of the uncoiling motion on the serve. That's a source of power; plus it can guarantee that you'll go up to meet the ball, not wait for it to come down too low.

If this photo sequence showed my old serve, I'd be in a far different position at this point than I am below. I wouldn't be leaning forward; in fact, my back would be arched over backward to hit the ball over my head.

As you can see, my new toss lets me lean into the court for power and comfort.

6

LET YOUR MOMENTUM CARRY YOU INTO THE COURT

At contact with the ball (8), I'm in absolute control of the point. I've snapped my forearm and wrist into the ball to give my serve good pace. Also, notice the position of the ball out in front of me. If that ball were to drop, it would land about a foot and a half inside the baseline.

It's the ball's position at contact that now allows me to serve with a lot more variety than ever before. I can go for a few more big flat ones as well as slice the ball wider to the backhand side . . . in short, I get a lot more punch.

Finally, I think that what happens immediately after you hit the ball is just as important as what goes on before. Your follow-through has a large bearing on the power and effectiveness of the serve. It should also carry you a step into the court.

So you can't afford to slow down your swing just after you've hit the ball. If you do, you'll rob your serve of power and accuracy. That means your opponent may be able to hit a more aggressive return.

My racquet head still carries plenty of speed after the ball has been hit (9 and 10). At this stage of my career, I can use a little more zip on my serves to win a few free points a match. Perhaps you can, too.

THE RETURN OF SERVE: MAINTAIN AN AGGRESSIVE ATTITUDE

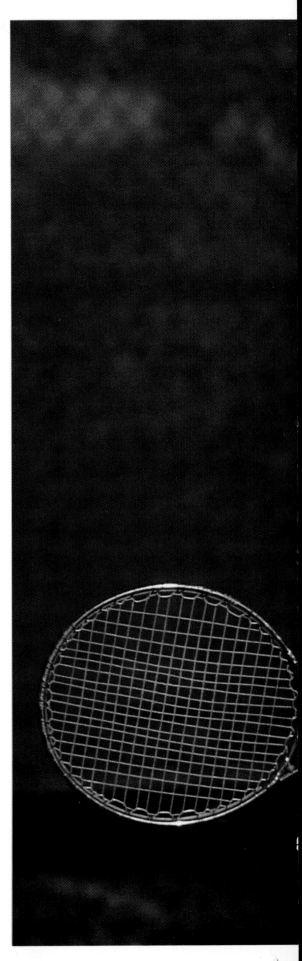

A lot of players are filled with confidence when they step up to the baseline to serve the ball. But turn the tables around and often you find quite a different story. Suddenly placed on the receiving end of a serve, they unknowingly put their bold, aggressive instincts on hold and become more tentative or defensive-minded. It's almost as if they've been conditioned to think that way after hearing for years that the server is the one who's supposed to control the start of a point.

That's probably where I've enjoyed the biggest edge over my opponents throughout my career. I never think defensively when I'm returning serve. I always try to do something extra with my return, to make it a strong counterattacking weapon so that even the biggest servers feel a little uneasy when they step to the line. They know they're in for a battle to hold serve, and that knowledge puts more pressure on them.

At the club level, that kind of aggressive attitude on service returns could pay off for you, too—and in a big way. So I'd like to spell out my return-of-serve philosophy for you and outline the major stroking keys that should help you neutralize the server's natural advantage at the start of a point.

Practice, of course, is the surest route to developing a solid, attacking return of serve. In fact, when I was about 12 years old, I routinely got a unique type of workout that really made my service return the effective weapon it is today.

During the winter, I used to play indoors on

An offensive outlook: I never think defensively when I'm returning serve (right). I'm always trying to pressure the server.

You have to stay alert to handle anything they throw your way.

wooden boards at the National Guard Armory in St. Louis, Mo. To say the unusual courts were fast would be an understatement because maintenance people waxed and polished the floors often for military marching exercises. The result? Balls would skid and accelerate after they bounced.

I remember that the pro I played there always used to serve wide into the deuce court. As a matter of fact, he served so wide with slice that at first he was running me from Court 3 all the way to Court 1! I laid down so much rubber in retrieving his serves, I quickly learned that the only way to take control of the point was to move in and meet the ball early after the bounce.

The proper type of practice should serve as the basis of your service returns as well. For example, if you play on soft clay courts 90 percent of the time and you're scheduled to compete in a tournament on hard courts, there's little chance you'll be able to handle a powerful server on the fast surface unless you prepare. My advice is to find a court that plays the same in speed and have a practice partner serve to you from a few feet inside his baseline. I guarantee you'll be working like mad at first, but you'll quickly learn to control your stroke and move your feet more efficiently.

Once you've got the basics under control, you should look to match experience to raise the effectiveness of your returns to another level. By facing players over and over again, you should be able to pick out serving patterns that will allow you to get better prepared for a return.

I like to pay particular attention to my opponent's serving strategy in certain game situations. Does he ease up on his serve when he's under a lot of pressure? Does he usually serve wide or come right at me when he's down 0-15 or 0-30 in his service game? The answers to these kinds of questions can help create an important service break just when I need it.

Although I'm careful to keep track of an opponent's serving strategy in a match, I think that my being able to "read" his service toss may be the biggest key to my success with service returns. I get important hints about the type, speed and direction of the serve that's about to come at me by watching where the ball is placed in respect to the server's body on the toss, as well as how his racquet comes through the ball at contact. I know those observations came in handy on the boards in St. Louis!

For instance, if your opponent releases the ball in front of his body but out toward the side, you can bet he's going to come around it with slice. If the ball's more directly out in front, the chances are he'll serve a hard, flat one. And a toss behind the head is almost a sure giveaway for a kick or twist serve.

Reading an opponent's toss requires split-second analysis and quick reactions on your part. You don't have a lot of time to think on court, so the technique should be made nearly instinctive through practice.

And, of course, it's far from foolproof. Some players, for example, can hit a variety of serves off the same toss. Others are harder to read, in my opinion, because they have what I call a "floating" toss. They don't have control of their toss, so the ball tends to move around from one serve to the next at random. They're nearly impossible to read. You just have to stay mentally alert to handle anything they throw your way.

While the right type of practice and match experience provide the basics for developing an effective return of serve, a proper mental attitude is the factor that welds them together to create a reliable weapon.

Although my many years of experience have taught me to throw in

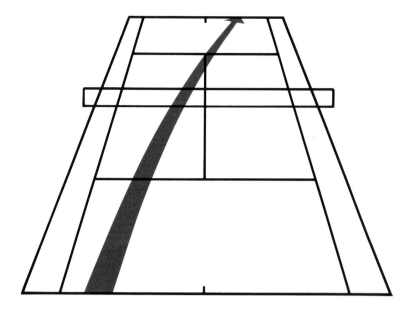

RETURN OF
SERVE OPTIONS...

Vs. Baseliners: It's very hard to hit a clean winner off the serve. So your best bet is to send your return deep to put your opponent's back against the wall.

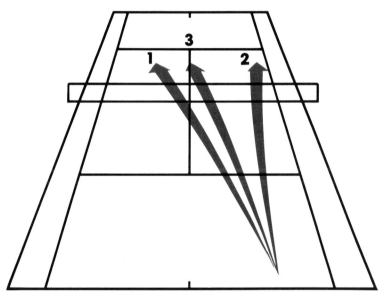

Vs. Serve-and-Volleyers: These players give you specific targets to aim for on your return. Try to pass them left or right (1 and 2), or hit right at their feet (3).

occasional changes of pace on my returns, I still like to go for winners whenever I get the chance. And it's not a low-percentage play for me because I'm often able to anticipate serves and adjust my position so that I can put all of my weight into the return.

Now I'm not suggesting that you shoot for the lines on your service returns, but you should have a definite purpose or plan in mind when you're waiting for the serve to be hit. Even if you're crossed up on the serve and you have to throw your plan out the window, it's a help more often than not.

I find that I return best against serve-and-volleyers because they give me definite targets to aim for when they rush the net—off to the sides or at their feet. It's much harder to hit a winning return against baseliners because they can run down balls in the backcourt.

So regardless of the type of opponent you're facing, have a target in mind before the serve is hit. There will be times when you'll be forced to stick your racquet out, hold on tight and hope for the best. But when you can manage a solid return, you'll have just as good a chance of winning the point as your opponent does.

Now, turn the page for a look at the stroking keys that are sure to add a little more offensive punch to your service returns.

KEYS TO THE RETURN OF SERVE

ATTACK YOUR OPPONENT'S SERVE

You don't stand a chance of hitting a solid, attacking return of serve unless you get into good position to meet the ball quickly (see photo 1 below). Fortunately, that's one of my greatest strengths.

Good racquet preparation is another essential when you've got a powerful serve bearing down on you. As the ball approaches (2), I'm completing a shoulder pivot sideways to the net. That move accomplishes two things. First, it gets my racquet back. And second, it coils my body for a more powerful forward stroke.

Whether I'm hitting a forehand or backhand return, I keep both hands on the racquet to help me bring it back swiftly. And while I'm setting up for a service return, I have but one simple thought: Move forward and into the court. Why? Too many players allow themselves to be pushed around by average serves.

Right from the start, I position myself close to the baseline so that I can easily move in toward the net. Then, I go after the ball (3). I advance at an angle to cut off the ball as it rises.

3

4

UNCOIL YOUR UPPER BODY INTO THE SHOT

The big payoff for good racquet preparation and footwork on the return of serve comes at the point of impact with the ball. When everything falls into place, you can make solid contact out in front of your body (4) and drill the ball back to put the server on his heels.

The power of my returns comes from the quick uncoiling action of my upper body. I rotate my shoulders into the shot (5) to generate more pace.

A full follow-through (6) is the natural extension of my compact, but powerful, stroking style.

It gives me control on my returns. I'll use a longer finish on the stroke if I'm going for a winner on a hard court or if I'm playing on clay, where I generally have more time to recover after my return. On a really fast court, though, I'll shorten my follow-through slightly in order to prepare more quickly for my next shot.

5

6

THE VOLLEY: MAKE EVERY ONE COUNT

In a military battle, the most devastating, effective weapons are often the ones that are underestimated or overlooked. From firsthand experience, I can tell you that the same holds true on a tennis court.

For example, ground strokes and baseline play have generally been the best-known parts of my game. As a result, my volleys never get much attention. But I think my net play has been largely responsible for the success I've enjoyed in the game, especially in the last few years.

Granted, I'm not the type of player who goes to the net and feels comfortable hitting three, four or five volleys in a row while lunging from side to side. My route to the net is usually behind a solid approach shot or ground stroke. In fact, I play my approaches hard and close to the lines so that it makes it tough for my opponent to hit a good passing shot.

The result? I often end points with one volley. There's no cute stuff; I get the job done quickly. I like to pick off any ball above waist level and put everything I have behind it for a winning volley. That rattles opponents because they know I won't come to the net behind a mediocre shot. They know they're going to have to thread the needle with a passing shot or they're in trouble.

Adding a similar net dimension to your game at the club level can be just as effective and intimidating. It can lift the level of your play a notch or two above the rest of the competition because most of your opponents probably rely on a one-dimensional style of play. Here are some ideas that may start you on your way to developing a respected net attack.

Your first, and probably most important, step should be to make an honest assessment of your game's strengths and weaknesses. For example, if you've clung to the baseline like a security blanket for years, don't try to become a

An aggressive attitude: I like to pick off any ball above waist level (right) and put everything I have behind it for a winning volley.

I *often end points with one volley. There's no cute stuff; I get the job done quickly.*

volleying master at the net overnight. Work your way gradually into a more aggressive playing style.

I prefer to hit a minimum number of solid volleys whenever I reach the net because that approach fits in well with the rest of my game. I'll hit a soft angled volley or drop volley on occasion, but only when I have to meet the ball below the level of the net or when my opponent is way out of position.

If your game is more oriented toward finesse shots, you have other options that can make you just as effective at the net. Ilie Nastase, for example, didn't sting his volleys, but still rates as one of the game's best net players.

Why? He had an excellent serve, quick hands and fast reflexes. Because he opened up the court so much with his serves, he could often afford to use more touch on his volley.

Another key to successful net play is good anticipation—whether you're constantly forcing the issue from the net or sneaking in from the baseline occasionally to keep your opponents guessing.

I think of anticipation as having a feel for the total point and game situation when you move into your forecourt. In other words, knowing what your opponent is likely to try (given his stroking ability and position on the court) and where to move to cut off his angles for a successful passing shot.

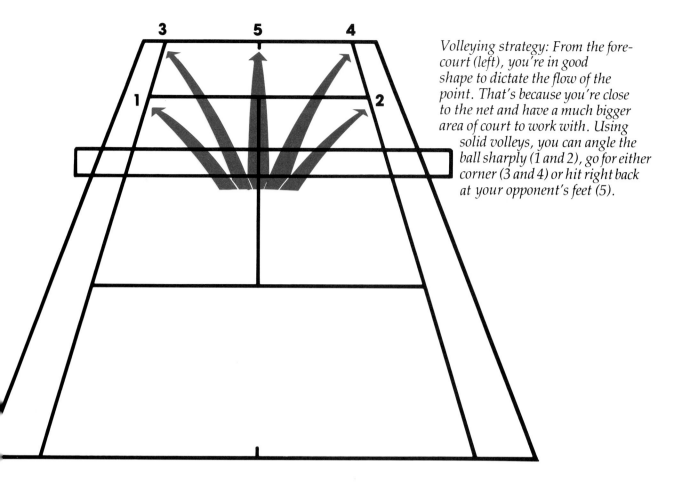

Volleying strategy: From the fore-court (left), you're in good shape to dictate the flow of the point. That's because you're close to the net and have a much bigger area of court to work with. Using solid volleys, you can angle the ball sharply (1 and 2), go for either corner (3 and 4) or hit right back at your opponent's feet (5).

Anticipating shots: Your work at the net (left) will be much simpler if you're able to develop a feel for what your opponent is likely to try, given his stroking ability and position on the court.

For instance, if I hit an angled approach that really makes my opponent stretch out wide of the sideline, I'll look for him to go down the line with his passing shot. That's his best option. He'd have to make one heck of a return to flip the ball crosscourt for a winner. So I'll adjust my position toward the sideline to anticipate the more likely return. Most of the time, I'll have a lot of open court where I can place my volley.

And if my opponent runs down my approach within the court, it helps to know his shot tendencies and how he reacts under the pressure of my rushing the net. Does he panic? Or does he stay cool, pick a target and go for his shot? This type of knowledge comes as the result of match experience. You should make a real effort to file away bits and pieces of information on other players.

Finally, footwork can either make or break you at the net. I always keep my feet moving with tiny steps so that I can push off easily and quickly in any direction to cut off a return.

For me, getting into a balanced volleying position is crucial because it allows me to uncoil and spring into my volleys. Good footwork lets me do a lot of things with the ball: I can put more sting on the volley, move in and angle it toward the sideline, or just drive it deep.

Remember, develop an all-court game and visit the net as often as you can. Once you're there, make your volleys count!

KEYS TO THE FOREHAND AND BACKHAND VOLLEYS

TURN SIDEWAYS EARLY

My main strength at the net comes from an overall feel for the flow of points and an ability to anticipate my opponent's shots. As a result, I'm always ready to react quickly and instinctively.

The key to my volley preparation is an immediate shoulder turn sideways to the ball's line of flight. I make this move as soon as the ball leaves my opponent's racquet.

A good shoulder turn for both my forehand volley (see sequence photos above right) and backhand volley (below right) accomplishes three things. First, it coils my upper body so that I can really sting the ball (1). Second, it automatically brings my racquet back as far as needed(2); I don't have to waste time with a longer backswing. And third, it sets me up to push off quickly to reach wide balls (3).

You can see in both sequences on the right that I'm now in good shape to meet the ball on my terms. Because I didn't delay in reacting to my opponent's passing shot attempt, I'll be able to dictate the action with my volley.

THE FOREHAND VOLLEY

THE BACKHAND VOLLEY

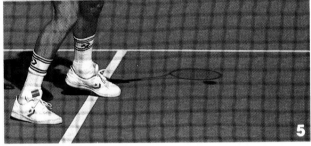

MAKE CONTACT OUT IN FRONT OF YOUR BODY

If you prepare properly and keep your racquet motion compact, making solid contact with the ball is fairly easy. I always try to hit the ball out in front of my body (see photos 4 and 5 above and below), before it passes my front shoulder. The reason for that is simple: Once the ball gets behind you, you tend to lose control of your volley. Sure, you might still be able to get the ball back across the net, but your volley won't have much pace.

What should the volleying motion look like? Under ideal conditions, your racquet head should move slightly downward, at an angle, through impact. This type of stroke puts some backspin on the ball and keeps it low to the court after the bounce. But if I'm close to the net and the ball's above waist level, I'll often just come through it with a flat stroke. The amount of pace on that type of volley is enough to keep the ball low.

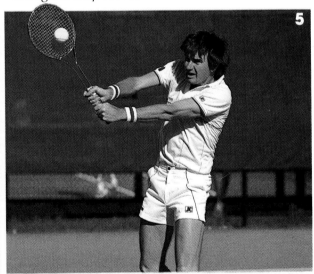

6

7

FINISH YOUR VOLLEYS AGGRESSIVELY

Although I don't come into contact with as many club players as a career teaching pro does, I have noticed that a widespread problem is a lack of aggressiveness.

In my matches, I can't afford to ease up on the ball just to get it back in play, and neither can you if you're facing a tough opponent. So I concentrate on hitting through each ball on my volleys, and a good follow-through is an indication of that (6 and 7).

Although your follow-through has to be compact to give you time to recover for your next volley, you shouldn't cheat yourself out of hitting the ball solidly by starting to slow down your racquet head too soon. My attitude is, if I hit the ball in the middle of my racquet firmly enough, my opponent probably won't have time to hit an offensive shot, so I'll have a fraction more time to recover into a good ready position. Think the same way, and I guarantee you'll close out more points at the net.

6

7

THE DEFENSIVE LOB: USE IT TO BUY TIME

'll bet you and I have a lot more in common in terms of our tennis games than you might imagine. Sure, we both love the game with all its excitement and action, but if you're a typical club player, you probably don't use the defensive lob as often as you should.

I remember that while I was a youngster growing up in the St. Louis area, I didn't have much use for a defensive lob either. My success was based on my powerful ground game, as it still is today. And my power was enough to win plenty of my matches.

Whenever an opponent put me on the defensive with a shot, I would always try to respond offensively, relying on my ground strokes to bail me out of trouble. Even at that young age, my preference for playing all-out, hard-nosed tennis had become ingrained in my mind. I guess I was just too stubborn to admit that my opponent had gotten the better of me with a particular series of shots.

But all that changed somewhat when I played tennis at UCLA. For the year that I was on the team, coach Glenn Bassett emphasized the importance of the lob. Of course, that message wasn't news to me. I had heard it many times before. But when your coach makes you work on your lobs in two-on-one drills day after day, the skills tend to stay with you despite your stubbornness.

Coach Bassett's influence, plus the fact that I was playing bigger, tougher, faster players than ever before, helped me realize that there are times when

A point-saver: The defensive lob may not be an aggressive shot, but it has its place in even the most powerful player's game.

There are times when you have to put aside your desire to play an aggressive shot.

Give the ball a ride: Because the ball must go so high and deep, be sure to stroke through the ball fully (right).

you have to put aside your desire to play an aggressive shot and opt instead for a defensive lob. With the lob at least, you buy the chance to stay in the point for another shot, a chance you might not get if you attempted a lower percentage return.

Although I still prefer to hit aggressive shots whenever possible, the message I learned about the defensive lob at UCLA has stuck with me. In fact, the power of my ground game leads many inexperienced opponents to overlook or underestimate the effectiveness of my lob. When that happens, my defensive lob becomes almost an offensive weapon.

The most important thing to remember when hitting a defensive lob is to make sure you send the ball high and deep. You're simply trying to buy some time to get back into decent court position. And when you're scrambling like mad to reach an opponent's shot, that's about all you'll have time to think of.

But the top players always have a purpose in mind on all shots, even the defensive lob. For example, when I'm forced way out of position, I'll usually hit my lob crosscourt for two reasons. First, it's in the air longer,

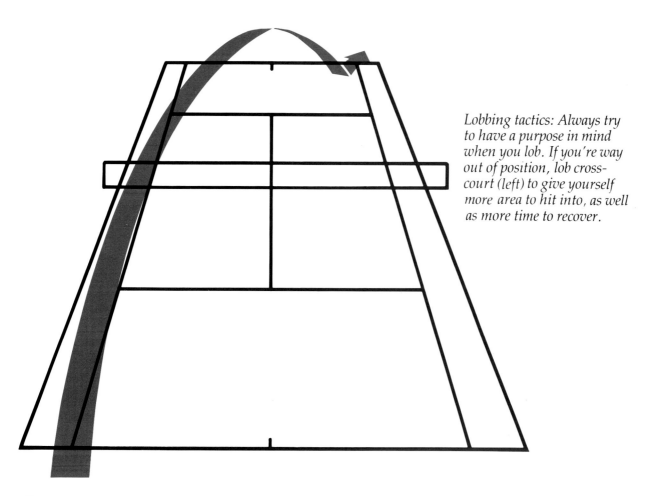

Lobbing tactics: Always try to have a purpose in mind when you lob. If you're way out of position, lob cross-court (left) to give yourself more area to hit into, as well as more time to recover.

allowing me more time to get back into the middle of the backcourt. Second, the distance the ball travels is farther, so I have more court to work with on the shot.

As for stroking technique, I think that the two most important elements are good preparation and a full follow-through. If you take care of these priorities, the rest of the stroke pretty much falls into place automatically.

Obviously, another critical element in hitting a great lob is to get a quick jump on your opponent's shot. If you're able to reach the ball with a split second to spare, the accuracy of your lob will improve tremendously because you'll be less rushed. On the other hand, if your reactions are slow, you may have to resort to a flick of the wrist . . . and a quick prayer that your lob won't fall short.

The best way to get a jump on an opponent's forcing shot is to run naturally with your racquet at your side. If you take it back too soon, you'll reduce your speed. I only take my racquet back when I get within close range of the ball. Even then, it's only a short backswing.

Despite the compact backswing, I'm able to stroke through the ball fully to send it high and deep. My swing is simple, and yours should be, too. Just remember to finish the stroke with a complete follow-through. If you try to cut it short to get back into position a little more quickly, your lob is likely to fall short as well and your opponent's winning overhead will be a blur.

So the next time your instructor or coach suggests you work on your defensive lob, jump at the opportunity. It may not be an aggressive shot, but it has its place in even the most powerful player's game. I should know.

KEYS TO THE DEFENSIVE LOB

RUNNING DOWN THE BALL

As soon as I see that my opponent's shot is going to be trouble, I pivot and begin running like a sprinter with my arms pumping at my sides (see photo 1 below). If I were to start my racquet back too early, I wouldn't be able to run as quickly.

It's only when I get within a few steps of reaching the ball (2) that I begin my backswing. Notice that my eyes are fixed on the ball throughout my preparation. Because my opponent's shot is moving away from me and at an angle, I need to keep it in my sights.

When I get near the spot where I'm going to make contact, my backswing is complete. I keep it short (3) so that timing the hit won't be a problem.

3

POWER YOUR RACQUET THROUGH THE BALL

My forward swing is a smooth one, from low to high (4 and 5). A lot of players hit their defensive lobs with underspin, which has a tendency to make balls hang in the air. But I prefer to hit the ball almost flat, with little spin. My attitude is: Keep the lob as simple as possible. From your defensive position off the court, you're not in good enough shape to do anything fancy with the ball.

The ideal defensive lob sails high in the air and lands just inside your opponent's baseline. Think about how far the ball must travel to accomplish those twin objectives. To get that kind of depth on your lob, you must swing through the ball completely and not cut short your stroke. My follow-through (6 and 7) serves as an indication that I've given the ball a good ride. Next, I'll quickly recover my position near the middle of the backcourt in the hope of getting another shot opportunity.

THE OVERHEAD: EMPHASIZE PLACEMENT OVER POWER

I f you're like me, a defensive lob is a welcome sight during any point. It means you've successfully outmaneuvered your opponent with a series of shots that have backed him into a corner from which there's little chance of escape. Your job's not over, though. You still have to finish off the point with your overhead. Sure it looks easy, and you may think the point is like money in the bank. But I've seen many players—even pros—blow the overhead simply because they try to do too much with the shot. While the ball is on its way down, they may be thinking how impressive it would be to blast the ball off the court so it bounces 10 rows deep in the bleachers. That attitude can be costly.

I like to think of my overhead as more of a workhorse-type stroke. It's not fancy and it won't win a lot of prizes for power, but it rarely lets me down. It's dependable and effective. That's all I need in an overhead. You can probably upgrade your overhead, too, by toning down the emphasis on power and focusing instead on placement.

Aside from the stroking basics I always try to follow (see the photo sequence that follows), I think the biggest keys to the success of my overhead are alertness and quick preparation. Against most players, I'm able to pick up the ball early as it comes off the racquet and start moving into position quickly. Other players, though, don't telegraph their lobs as much. They'll just give you a little flick of the wrist to get the ball up over you. That's where staying on your toes really pays off.

Of course, knowing your opponent's ability and what he likes to do under certain conditions can help give you a split-second edge in reaction time as well. For example, if your approach shot or volley is good enough to force your opponent to move at an angle backward, away from his baseline, you should realize he doesn't have much of a shot at passing you. Because his momentum is away from the net and the ball has to travel so far to reach you, you'll probably be able to pick off such a shot with a winning volley. The only smart bet your opponent has is a lob, so you should watch for it.

Another important thing to consider as you get in position to hit an

Stay awake at the net: The biggest keys to the success of my overhead are alertness and quick preparation (right). I'm always ready to move back.

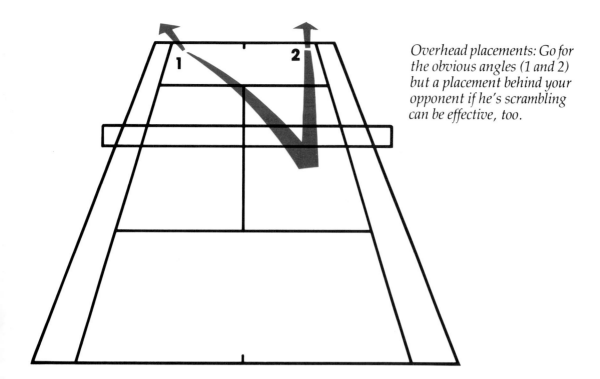

Overhead placements: Go for the obvious angles (1 and 2) but a placement behind your opponent if he's scrambling can be effective, too.

overhead is the type of spin your opponent has put on the lob. If the ball has topspin, it will drop out of the air more sharply and quickly. So don't wait until the last second to bring your racquet back or you'll have to rush your swing. You have to prepare earlier to hit an overhead off a topspin lob.

A defensive, underspin lob, on the other hand, tends to float in the air, so good overheads require a little more patience on your part. Early preparation, of course, is still important, but you have to be careful not to pull the trigger on your overhead too soon or the ball's likely to catch the top edge of your racquet.

In the heat of battle, I know it can be tough to control your eagerness when you see that weak lob fly into the air. The better players bide their time and pick off lobs with overhead winners almost routinely. You should try to develop the same type of patient, businesslike attitude.

While I'm patient on my overheads, I like to hit the ball before it bounces, provided the lob isn't too deep. That's because I don't want to give my opponent any extra time to get into a better return position behind his baseline.

There aren't any great secrets to placing the overhead. Most of the time, you're going to hit it away from your opponent. Even if he's able to run down the ball, the chances are he won't be able to do too much with his return. But what I like to do occasionally is hit behind my opponent, especially on a clay court, because he'll probably be scrambling to cover the open corner of his court. He'll have a tough time putting on the brakes to retrieve the ball.

So keep in mind that there are two ways to hit an overhead. You can go for the spectacular smash, which attracts a lot of attention but produces more than its share of mis-hits, or you can fire a solid, but controlled, overhead that will win points consistently. To my mind, the choice is easy.

Smart preparation: Take your racquet up and back early (left) to eliminate rushed swings.

KEYS TO THE OVERHEAD

LIFT YOUR RACQUET UP AND BACK QUICKLY

When an opponent sends up a high, defensive lob, he's telling you he's in big trouble. You've got to react quickly and efficiently to take advantage of the situation.

The first step in hitting a solid overhead is to turn sideways to the lob's line of flight (see photo 1 below). Then, I get my racquet up and back early—there's no time for a full service-type motion—and move into position a bit behind where I think the ball will drop (2).

Finally, as the ball comes into hitting range, I start my upward swing from behind my back (3).

3

4

EXTEND YOUR BODY THROUGH CONTACT

The overhead is an aggressive shot, so you've got to go after the ball (4)and meet it with your body fully extended . If you wait for the ball to get too low, you won't get as much leverage on your shot.

Notice in photo 5 that the momentum of my racquet head through impact with the ball is continuing forward at a good pace. This racquet movement ensures a full upper-body pivot that adds to the force of my overhead.

I complete the stroke with a full follow-through on the opposite side of my body (6). My weight is forward at this point and I'm ready to move in, anticipating a weak return from my opponent.

HOW TO HANDLE
TOUGH HIGH &
LOW BALLS

f the laws of physics were changed so that every return hit during a match bounced to you consistently at waist level, you'd have it made, right? After all, it would be fairly easy to groove your ground strokes if all of your opponent's shots came right down the pipe. The ball would be in an ideal hitting zone and you'd be in perfect balance.

Of course, that's not what happens on court. Your opponent isn't going to spoon-feed you returns. He's going to attempt to work you over with a variety of shots and spins, and try to make you run madly from corner to corner. And because there are so many good players around today, both pros and amateurs, it's essential to be well-rounded with your strokes.

If you're looking to strengthen your ground attack, my advice is to work hard on your returns of high balls and low balls. I think that practice in these two areas alone could elevate your game quickly. Here's a look at what I consider the essentials of the two types of returns. →

Delivering low blows: Always play low returns with a definite purpose in mind. Get down to the level of the ball (above) and then follow through completely on the shot.

High-level tactics: Take your racquet back high (left) and keep a firm grip as you lean into the shot.

Handling the high bouncer: Take a high backswing (1), keep a firm grip (2) and lean into the shot (3).

THE HIGH BOUNCER: LEAN INTO THE SHOT

When I was coming up through the junior ranks, most of the guys I played with—such as Dick Stockton, Roscoe Tanner, Brian Gottfried, and Sandy and Gene Mayer—preferred to hit the ball flat or with slice.

Not long after reaching the pros, though, I was introduced to the extreme topspin ground strokes of Bjorn Borg and Guillermo Vilas. Their high-kicking returns demanded that I make some adjustments in my strokes. I tried to take their shots on the rise at waist level whenever I could in order to be aggressive. But occasionally, I'd have to return their balls at shoulder height.

The basics I followed to make my high returns a strength of my attack can do the same for you. Here they are.

The first essential in handling a high-bouncing ball is a backswing that positions your racquet head slightly above the level where you plan to make contact with the ball (see photo sequence above). If you try to put topspin on a ball at shoulder level by starting with a low backswing, you're making a mistake. There's no way you'll be able to hit a shot with any pace.

Next, don't react defensively to the kicker. Be aggressive and go after the ball by leaning into the shot. Swing forward at an angle to meet the ball in front of your body and give it a solid ride. The underspin that you'll put on the ball with such a swing will keep the ball low in your opponent's court.

I've also found that it pays to keep a firm grip through contact, especially for one-handed shots, because the heavy spin on kickers can knock the racquet loose. That's probably the reason why my high two-handed backhand returns are more offensive than my forehands. The extra hand I've got on my grip helps stabilize the racquet at impact.

As for placement, my ability to play high returns gives me a number of options that I can rely on in pressure situations. If I'm near the baseline, I can push the ball deep to set up my next return. And if I'm inside the court, I can direct the ball to either corner or angle it short.

Wouldn't you like to have such a weapon in your arsenal? Practice and hard work are the answer. Don't let topspinners and moonballers get the better of you!

Because there are so many good players around today, it's essential to be well-rounded with your strokes.

THE COURT-HUGGER: GET DOWN AND HIT OUT

Several years ago when topspin was the buzzword in professional tennis, the effectiveness of the underspin shot that hugs the court after it bounces was largely overlooked, especially by fans. But with the comeback of the serve-and-volley and more aggressive styles of play, the slice shot has become more popular, even at the club level.

What's the most effective way to return a low ball?

I wish I could tell you there's an easy way to reach such a shot. If there were, it would certainly make my life a lot easier on the tour.

But effort is the key to a successful return of a low shot. And the first step in that effort is getting down for the ball by bending at the knees and waist (see photo sequence below). One of my first objectives on low-ball returns is to get my head low enough so that I have the same perspective in watching the ball approach that I would on a waist-high shot. That makes it easier for me to time my swing.

While I'm bending down to reach the ball, I prepare early by turning my shoulders sideways to the net and taking a compact backswing. If you use a large, looping backswing for waist-level balls, you'll probably find that you make more errors on low returns because such a backswing is tougher to control when you're hunched over for the shot.

It's also important to follow through fully after you've made solid contact for good depth and pace. A short, choppy swing usually produces the type of weak, floating shot that an aggressive player will jump all over.

Finally, get in position quickly to return a low shot. I've always found that getting set early helps me hit out on the ball with a purpose. That's the name of my game. Make it the trademark of yours, too.

Returning the court-hugger: Get your body low (1), take a simple backswing (2) and hit out on the ball (3).

Low-risk changes-of-pace: I use my outside-in ground strokes (backhand above) like a baseball pitcher. I mix them in with powerful shots to keep opponents off balance.

CHANGE PACE TO KEEP AN OPPONENT HONEST

During his great years in boxing, Muhammad Ali once said, "Only a fool is not afraid of a crazy man."

I've always remembered that remark. In fact, on the tennis court, I've thought of myself as being the kind of crazy man Ali was talking about—crazy in terms of my game, my attitude. For most of my career, my whole approach was just to go forward. It was the way I enjoyed playing and what the people came out to see. In short, I played with reckless abandon.

So up until a couple of years ago, I played at only one pace. I always hit out with power. Everything clicked. I was young and had so much confidence in my game that I could go at this pace for four hours if I had to. Right at the beginning of a match, I'd try to jump on top of an opponent and keep pounding away at him. I wouldn't let up.

But you may have noticed that my game has changed slightly in the last year or two. I've learned to mix it up every once in a while, to change the pace. I feel I can bide my time more in a match now, so I don't start out against an opponent at such a hurried, powerful pace. Instead, I kind of go with the flow of the match for a while and feel out my opponent before turning on the real power.

You're probably thinking that the change of philosophy may be a result of old age setting in. But I don't look at it that way. My game is still based on raw power. If I get a chance to win a point with either a cute touch shot or a solid drive, you know which one I'll choose.

I'm still a young car, as far as style and attitude are concerned; I've just been through four engines in my career. So my years of experience out there on the tour have taught me to add a few new dimensions to my game to keep the engine I've got now running smoothly. Now, I'm changing pace a little more often and using some variety in my shots. I also take more time to settle down between points.

Overall, I'd say that's a good approach for any experienced player to take, especially at the club level. It's just a part of the learning process. You should get wiser as you get older.

Patience is one of the keys to changing a game that's based so much on

Added dimensions: I'll occasionally throw in a drop shot (above left) to set up a winner and hit a high looper when I'm winded in a point (right).

power. My children, Brett and Aubree Leigh, have had a lot to do with helping me develop my patience. They've taught me to temper my emotions. And with that patience has come a little more variety. I mix up my shots and don't hit the ball with the same speed all the time . . . not just going boom, boom, boom. Instead, I look for more control sometimes. I think that's one of the reasons for my success. I've been giving myself more of a chance on shots, more margin for error sometimes.

The three shots that I use to change pace during points are outside-in ground strokes, high loopers with a little topspin and drop shots. The first two are high-percentage strokes for me and the third, although it's riskier, probably isn't quite as dangerous as usual because of the situations in which I use it.

Patience is one key to changing a game based so much on power.

My outside-in ground strokes (Chapter 20) are like curveballs that I sometimes throw in with my fastballs or solid ground strokes. Rather than drive straight through the ball, I swing so that my racquet head brushes across the back of the ball with a slicing, sideways motion. The result is a slower-moving spin shot that curves as it flies across the net and bounces toward the corner.

I usually hit the shot from around the center of my baseline, so that I can slide the ball into one of my opponent's corners to force him wide of the court. Often, it will give me a big opening to hit into with my next shot.

The second change-of-pace shot I occasionally rely on is a high looper that I hit the same way as an offensive lob (Chapter 18). I think I really started using it a few years ago at the French Open on the slow clay. In fact, I remember that the first few times I tried the looper, I felt embarrassed. I said to myself, "Geez, how can you do that? You're not supposed to play like that! That's not your game." Then, I'd go out and I'd see Bjorn Borg, Guillermo Vilas, Ilie Nastase and a bunch of other guys do it five or six times a point. It took quite a while to reach a point where the looper felt comfortable in my game.

Now when I'm in a long rally, especially when I'm tired, I'll use the looper, too, for a drastic change of pace. It gives me a little bit more time to get into good position for my next shot and it helps me catch my breath. I don't hit the ball with an exaggerated topspin motion. I just lift the ball with a little topspin because that reduces the chances of mistiming the shot.

The drop shot (Chapter 21) is my other change-of-pace shot, but I don't really use it to win points outright like most players. That's because I don't have the incredible touch of, say, a John McEnroe or a Nastase. I think that's a quality you're born with. You can't learn to develop it.

But I feel if my opponent is back against the fence, I can hit a decent drop shot and still get by with it. Often, the guy across the net will be barely able to reach the ball, so I'll follow-up the drop shot with another return that I hope will be a winner. I use the drop shot more to set up a point than to win it right away.

As I play more and more on the tour, I'm experimenting a little more with changing pace during rallies. Of course, my basic strategy is still simple: I hit powerful ground strokes from the baseline. Changing the pace once in a while during those kinds of rallies can startle opponents. A lot of players aren't used to seeing that from me, so it can cause a little bit of hesitation on their part when they go to make a return. The same approach can work for you.

I know I'm not going to win many points on a change-of-pace shot alone. But it makes the rest of my game that much more effective.

Don't get me wrong. I don't plan to slow down my whole game. When I'm finished in tennis, I want to go out with my big guns firing.

The lesson to be learned here is that small changes in your approach to the game can pay off in big ways. It took me quite a while to realize that, because my power game was strong. I was stubborn, but I wasn't stupid. By changing pace every now and then, I've added a whole new dimension to my attack. Maybe you can do the same.

HOW TO BE
QUICKER ON COURT

O nce in a while, I hear tennis writers compare my footwork to Ken Rosewall's. I don't know if the comparison fits because I never really watched his footwork. Whenever I played Rosewall, I was too busy chasing down balls to pay much attention to how he moved on court. But I'll say this: He always seemed to be in good position. He rarely hit a ball off balance. I'm usually able to get to balls early enough to set up for my shots, too. In fact, I think my footwork has been one of the biggest keys to the strength of my ground game.

There's no great secret to the way I move my feet on the tennis court. I just pick them up and lay them down and make sure they don't get tangled up in the process. I also have to admit I've never followed a running program or done any weight lifting to improve my footwork. It's 100 percent natural.

I find that because I play a lot of tournament matches, the amount of work I get is plenty to keep my footwork sharp. On off-weeks, though, I make sure I do a few agility drills after each day's practice to hold onto that edge. Because you probably don't get to play as much tennis as I do, you might want to try the footwork drills I describe on page 82 and even make them a part of your regular training routine. Here are some other thoughts I have about the importance of good footwork in a winning tennis game.

First, I think players are making a mistake if they feel raw speed is the only key to good footwork. Sure, it can help, especially when you have to chase down a ball in the opposite corner. But you rarely have to run more than a 10-yard dash out there and, most of the time, you don't even have to run that far.

The problem with raw speed is that it involves taking long strides. And when you're taking long strides, it's tough to make minor, but important, adjustments in position when you get near the ball. It's also tough to stop quickly and reverse directions. So you're really hurting in a match if you rely only on long strides to run down shots. →

Swift and sure: Small, sure steps form the
foundation of my footwork (left).

2 WAYS TO SHARPEN YOUR FOOTWORK

When I'm at home during a break in my playing schedule, I don't take my footwork for granted. After practice, I'll jump rope occasionally to keep the wheels in shape or do the drills I've outlined in the court diagrams below. They're designed to improve your quickness and agility, two things you should always work on in practice.

Try the drills yourself. They will wear you out after a good practice, but you'll soon see the benefits in your matches.

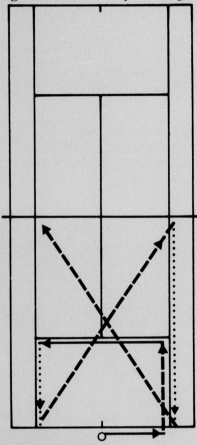

ALL-INCLUSIVE FOOTWORK DRILL

Using the lines of a tennis court, it's easy to set up your own drills to practice your footwork. I like to use the one shown in the diagram above because it combines sprinting, shuffling and backpedaling in a challenging pattern.

First, I shuffle sideways from the center of the baseline to the singles sideline. Then, I sprint up to the service line and shuffle crosscourt to the opposite sideline. From there, I backpedal to the baseline and follow that up with a sprint diagonally to the net, where I pause to towel off (just kidding). Next, I backpedal the length of the sideline and finish the drill with an all-out dash on an angle to the net.

CROSSCOURT WIND SPRINTS

To really get the blood flowing after practice, a few crosscourt wind sprints are just what the doctor ordered. Starting at the "T" of the service line (see the diagram above), I sprint to the singles sideline, touch it, then run crosscourt to the opposite singles sideline and touch it. I keep sprinting from sideline to sideline like this until I get winded.

KEY:
Regular sprint — — — — — —
Sideways shuffle ——————
Backpedal ....

I think you're better off having quickness and agility rather than raw speed.

While it's nice to have some speed, I think you're better off having quickness and agility. And that's where anticipation comes in, more or less knowing where the ball is going even before your opponent hits it. If you can anticipate an opponent's shot, then you get an important jump in taking your first step to run down the ball. From my own experience, I can tell you that your first step, if it's quick, is often the difference between getting to the ball early enough to set up for a solid shot or scrambling like crazy just to get your racquet on the ball.

Taking that quick first step requires a lot of coordination and good reflexes. First, your eyes have to pick up the ball right off your opponent's racquet. Then your brain has to tell your muscles to move. Your eyes, your mind and your body all have to work together in synch. Plus, you have to be relaxed so everything flows naturally.

I think that my ability to get a quick jump on the ball has helped me in many matches during my career. Even when I'm running down the most difficult of shots, I usually don't have to use more than two or three long strides. That's plenty to put me in a position where I can use the small, sure steps that form the foundation of my footwork on court. They're compact, just like the rest of my game.

If you watch me in a match, you'll see that I'm always moving my feet during a rally. Sometimes, I'll pick them up and lay them down just a few inches from where they were. But it's not wasted motion and energy. The constant movement has definite advantages. It keeps my weight on the balls of my feet so I'm always prepared; it lets me make very small, but important, adjustments in body position at the last second for more solid hits; and it makes it easier for me to push off and reverse directions after hitting the ball.

I can honestly say that after all these years, my feet have never failed me in a match. In fact, they've saved me a number of times when I've been a little bit run down. They keep moving, I keep winning. Work on your footwork so your feet won't fail you in your matches.

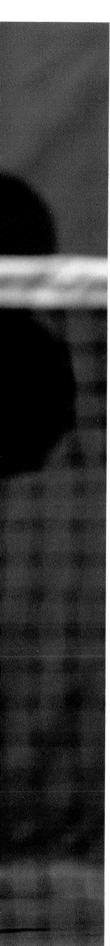

KEYS FOR GETTING TO THE NET

Labels can be deceiving when it comes to describing a player's style in tennis. Mention the term "baseliner," for example, and people tend to think of a player who stays back and hits ground strokes all day, who rarely attacks the net.

But just as the game has evolved to favor an all-court style of play today, so, too, have the games of most successful baseliners, including myself. Sure, I've won my share of matches from the backcourt against the game's best during my career. But I've never felt trapped back there. I'm always looking for a chance to get to the net. In fact, I think some of my biggest wins at the U. S. Open and Wimbledon were direct results of this philosophy.

Take my 1976 U.S. Open final against Bjorn Borg, for example. I practically wore a path to the net on critical points. At his best, Borg could keep opponents pinned to the back fence with his heavy topspin ground strokes. But his topspin returns started to fall short in that match, allowing me to move in, take the balls at shoulder height on the rise, drive them back deep to keep him on the run and win the title.

Since then, I find I'm sensing my opportunities to get to the net even better than I did in those days. There are two reasons. First, I'm not a youngster anymore. I'm looking to shorten points in order to make things a little easier on me over the course of a long match. Second, today's players are bigger, stronger and faster. The whole game has changed since I first began playing. Today, you need more of an all-court game to be a consistent winner.

At the club level, I'm sure the overall standard of play has followed a similar trend of improvement. You're undoubtedly discovering that in the trenches firsthand. So I'd suggest that you try to become more aggressive from the baseline, as I have, to keep a step or two ahead of the competition. Here are some thoughts that may help you go on the attack more successfully on court.

Unless you're a serve-and-volleyer who must naturally get to the net

Forcing the issue: I use my ground strokes to move my opponent around and force a weak return that I can jump on (left).

T*he whole game has changed. Today, you need more of an all-court game to be a consistent winner.*

quickly behind your deliveries, you'll have to work a little harder and a little longer to create openings for you to move in from the baseline. That requires some patience, plus a constant alertness, so that you don't fall asleep during long backcourt rallies, especially on clay courts. Too many players fall into that trap.

There isn't any great secret to the way I advance to the net. I simply use my ground strokes to move an opponent back and forth behind his baseline and, I hope, force a weak return that I can jump on, hit an approach shot and work my way to the service-court area close to the net.

The shots I'm always on the lookout for are short balls and floaters, textbook-type opportunities to move in provided you're offensive-minded. And regardless of who I'm playing, I know these chances will occur in every match. Generally, I'll force them with a solid series of shots. But I can also count on a few mis-hits by my opponent that will give me chances to attack. I've never been one to turn down those gifts, and neither should you.

When I'm not moving in on short balls and hitting approach shots off them or picking off floaters in the air with compact, volley-type strokes (see Chapter 17), I find another way to reach the net. How? By sneaking in. Since I'm not a serve-and-volley player, the element of surprise in attacking the net is crucial. I make sure my opponent keeps guessing about what I'm going to do.

Experience plays a vital role in determining the success of this tactic. You have to develop almost a sixth sense about it. For example, you might get the feeling that an opponent is easing up during a point or more or less taking a breather if the pace of your exchange is steady.

That's a time when I might try to startle him. After I hit the ball, I'll hesitate until I see that he's committed to his shot and then move in quickly to cut off the ball. If he doesn't see me run in, I have a good opportunity to hit a winning volley. And if he does see me out of the corner of his eye before he hits the ball, he may try to make a quick change in the direction of his shot and mis-hit. I think this type of approach would work well at the club level because players can really get flustered under such pressure.

Admittedly, hesitating at the baseline and sneaking in to the net behind a shot isn't the most common way of taking the offensive during a point. But it's effective.

So if you want to stay a step or two ahead of your competition, remember to make tracks to the net whenever you get a good opportunity. Don't forget to sneak in occasionally, too. You'll walk away with some easy points.

Sneaking in: The key to this tactic is hesitating at the baseline until you see that your opponent is committed to his shot (left).

MODIFY YOUR GAME TO SUIT DIFFERENT COURT SURFACES

The dimensions of a tennis court for singles play measure 36 feet by 78 feet. Yet even though those measurements never change, a tennis court has to rank right up there as one of the sports world's most changeable playing surfaces.

The reason? While you always compete against an opponent on a small, consistent piece of territory bordered by sidelines and baselines, the composition of that playing surface can vary drastically.

For starters, there are three types of court surfaces—grass, clay or man-made clay (like Har-Tru) and hard (asphalt or concrete). Next, every court, even those of the same type, varies in terms of speed. Red clay, for example, is undoubtedly the slowest playing surface, but it can be made to play even slower by adding more moisture to it. And hard courts can be made slicker than grass or as slow as clay by changing the composition and/or texture of the top coat of "paint."

Top off all of those variables with the fact that courts can be built indoors as well as outdoors, and you can begin to appreciate many of the adjustments that must be made constantly by tennis players who want to perform at their best. They must be flexible enough to modify their styles of play to suit different court surfaces.

In recent years, I've seen more and more pro players add that element of flexibility to their games. I believe the days are numbered for "specialists," those players who make names for themselves by playing most of the time on surfaces that favor their games. The pros now are more well rounded than ever before and I'm sure the trend is spreading down to the grass-roots level of the game as well. You shouldn't be left behind, so here's some advice that should help you hold your own against an opponent on any court surface.

The most important adjustment you must make when going from playing on one court surface to another is a mental one. The pro tour is divided into segments of sorts. For example, during the winter season, we'll play a lot of tournaments indoors on hard courts. Then, there's the French Open on red clay, a few events leading up to Wimbledon on grass and several more tournaments preceding the U.S. Open on hard courts.

As a club player, you probably find yourself locked into similar patterns of play on specific types of courts, with the exception of grass surfaces. You may play indoors on hard courts during the winter months and, in late spring, have to make a transition to playing on composition-clay courts at your club. Or if you live on the West Coast of the U.S. where hard courts

A true bounce: Because balls will usually take a predictable hop off a hard court, be aggressive (left).

Be prepared: Grass (above left) and clay courts (right) produce more than their share of unpredictable bounces.

are predominant, a vacation back East may find you at a resort that has only clay courts.

In any case, your first step in making a transition from one surface to another should be to keep in mind the playing differences you're sure to find between court surfaces. That piece of advice, I realize, sounds pretty obvious. Honestly, though, haven't you ever switched court surfaces and actually played a game or two before that fact hit you squarely between the eyes? It's so easy to become conditioned to playing on one type of court over a period of time, the problem is a common one.

Court speed and the type of bounce to expect should head your list of mental notes.

In general, clay courts are slow. The loose surface material bites into the ball when it bounces, slowing down even the hardest of serves and ground strokes. Ball bounces can also be erratic if shots catch a small mound of clay or the raised white tape of the court boundaries. In terms of footwork, remember that you have to slide into your shots on clay. If you try to use your normal footwork, particularly when you change direction, you'll find yourself sitting on your derriere.

On a hard court, whether it's carpeted or coated with a textured surface paint, you can generally expect the ball to reach you quickly after the bounce. But remember my warning about how these courts can be made to play fast or slow. You can determine a hard court's speed only by hitting on the court or talking with experienced players who've used it. As you'd expect, the bounce off most hard courts is true. About the only times it isn't are when the ball catches the seam of a carpeted court, which tends to kick the ball up to one side or another, or a painted line, which tends to make the ball skid.

I've left grass courts for last because not many players get the opportunity to play on this surface. However, it's still interesting to note its differences. First of all, not all grass courts are alike in playability. The grass at the Australian Open is not like that at Wimbledon, and neither is similar to the grass found at the West Side Tennis Club in Forest Hills, N.Y., former site of the U.S. Open. Even individual courts at Wimbledon seem to

T*he most important adjustment you must make when switching court surfaces is a mental one.*

have their own playing characteristics.

The bounce on grass courts is probably even more unpredictable than on clay because the turf wears down quickly with play, creating bald spots. Also, the bounce is usually quite low, so you have to have good footwork, and strong back and leg muscles, to get down to the ball throughout a match.

Once you've quickly reviewed the differences in play each court surface brings to the game, you need to think about how you can physically modify your style of play to increase your chances of winning. This step is what separates the specialists from the top all-court players.

If you have consistent, penetrating ground strokes and have a good bit of patience, you probably feel quite at home on a clay court. You can move your opponent around behind his baseline, relatively confident that he won't be able to hit many winners from the backcourt.

When you step onto a hard court, though, an aggressive opponent may eat you alive unless you have good passing shots. I recommend that you continue to work your opponent around the court with deep ground strokes. But you should stay alert for opportunities to move in to the net. You can do that off a weak return by hitting an approach or sneaking in behind one of your own strokes that's really put your opponent on the defensive. If you catch your opponent by surprise, you probably won't have to hit a terrific volley because there will be some open court to work with.

On the other side of the coin, if you're an attacking hard-court player who must make the transition to a clay court, you must realize that a lot of your offensive power will be taken away by the slower surface. You need more patience, not the type that would let you rally in long baseline duels, but the type that allows you to hang in there long enough to maneuver an opponent out of position. Then, you can go on the attack and close out the point.

The best way to achieve that goal is to take your opponent's shots on the rise, something I've always tried to do, and stay close to the baseline. If you don't, you'll probably get pinned way behind the baseline, especially if your opponent hits his ground strokes with heavy topspin.

I should also emphasize that serve-and-volleyers don't have to abandon their style of play totally on clay courts. If you've got that kind of a game, keep doing what you do best for most points. The key difference is that you must concentrate even harder on placing your serve more effectively because a powerful delivery won't be enough to pull you through tough matches on clay.

Finally, if you get the chance to play on grass, whatever your style of play, make sure your footwork is quick. You won't have much time to reach a lot of balls and they'll bounce low. Your best move is to keep alert and take the ball on the fly, before it bounces, whenever you can.

Being able to play well on all types of court surfaces should be a goal for every player. I can tell you that winning U.S. Open singles titles on three different surfaces—grass, Har-Tru and hard—has brought me a lot of personal satisfaction.

I've made some adjustments in my game to be successful and so can you. You've just got to believe in yourself and your ability in order to get the job done.

WINNING IS ALL IN THE MIND

I think that more than 95 percent of tennis at the pro level is mental. To be successful, you have to develop and maintain a positive attitude toward your game which, believe me, is a lot easier said than done under the immense pressures out there. That's because everybody on the tour these days plays good tennis.

But when it comes down to winning matches, it's usually not the great strokes, the aces or the net-cord winners that spell success. It's your mental approach—knowing what you *can* do, what you *should* do from a tactical standpoint and then *executing* your plan. To a large degree, winning is all in your mind.

Of course, I realize that in club play stroking ability plays a much bigger role in determining the outcome of matches. But if you're facing a player of equal ability, nine times out of 10 it's your mental attitude that will either leave you a frustrated loser or the guy who's holding the trophy after the last ball has been played. Now I'll outline my thinking on the mental side of the game. Maybe you'll be able to extract a few tips that will help you lift the level of your game.

As I've gotten older, my mental approach to tennis has changed. Coming up as a kid, I remember, there wasn't much pressure. There was nothing to lose. I was young and looking forward to playing the game's top stars. In fact, I still recall the first time I beat a tennis "legend." One of the guys I really looked up to was the Australian star, Roy Emerson, and I was fortunate enough to upset him when I was 17 years old in Los Angeles, the week after the U.S. Open in 1969.

In all fairness, it was probably tough for Emmo to get psyched up for our match after such a big event. Here he had to play a kid . . . but a kid who was eager as the devil. There came a point in that tight three-setter when I said to myself, "What the heck are you doing out here? You're just a kid but you've got a shot at beating one of the greats. Wake up! Wake up!"

Overcoming that moment of truth was a major stepping stone in my evolution as a player. There are a lot of established competitors out there, both pros and amateurs, who win a lot of matches just because of their reputations. It's kind of psychological intimidation; they don't do anything except walk out on the court and say "Hi" to their opponents, who are already soaked to the skin with sweat.

But the thing to remember when you're the underdog is that you've got the freedom to take chances and play all-out tennis. What a great

A winning edge: These days, you've got to play every match like it's the final.

Against a player of equal ability, your mental attitude will either leave you a frustrated loser or the guy who's holding the trophy.

position to be in! Sure, you have to deal with the nervousness of the moment and the challenge of facing a tough veteran. But just to be able to go out there and swing so fluently and aggressively . . . what I wouldn't give to be in that same position again!

After that first big win, I had to modify my mental approach to the game slightly. I won more and more matches, so I quickly went from being the underdog to the favorite. Fans' expectations and my own expectations shifted, requiring a change in my thinking.

For the most part, the change was the realization that I had to uphold my position in the rankings. I couldn't afford to let myself slip. I wasn't one of the hot young pursuers anymore, an upstart who could go for broke with little risk against more established players. I was the target, the guy the kids wanted to knock off.

I should emphasize that I didn't become more defensive on court. Instead, I made sure I stuck with a mental attitude that allowed me to play my own game, which has always included hitting out aggressively, attacking opponents and hustling for every shot.

Also, because lower-ranked players were gunning for me, I kept my guard up in the early rounds of tournaments. I knew that if I started looking ahead in the draw to a possible meeting with a seeded player, I could open up the door for a hungry youngster to come in and knock me off. In the old days, the top players might have been able to coast through a round or two before a real challenge. But these days, you've got to play every match like it's the final. That's a good playing philosophy for you to live by at the club level as well.

How do I psych myself up for a match?

Well, I'm from the old school. I just like to go out, serve 'em up and play. I'm sure you've heard of those new mental training techniques that some people support—like using mental images to see yourself playing and winning a match. I don't subscribe to any of those theories.

Because I'm familiar with the games of most of the players on tour, I never think far ahead about what I'm going to try to do in a match. I've found that if you sit down two nights before a match and start thinking about it, you'll drive yourself crazy. By the time you set foot on court, you're a bundle of nerves and jitters. That doesn't do a thing for your game; if anything, it detracts from your performance.

Before playing a tournament match, I just like to go off by myself somewhere private for five minutes or so to collect my thoughts. Sometimes, that can be difficult because there are usually so many guys hanging around the locker rooms, listening to loud music or joking around.

The key to my mental approach has been setting priorities. For example, when I'm off the court, tennis takes a back seat to my family and business

What's upstairs counts: Your mental approach to competition will often determine your success on court.

HOW TO READ
YOUR OPPONENT'S MENTAL CONDITION

A tough task: I had to grind it out against Bjorn Borg (above).

If you use your head alertly during a match, you can often pick up clues to an opponent's mental or emotional condition. These observations can help you devise a strategy that can swing the momentum of the match in your favor or even finish off your opponent.

I'm not talking about becoming a shrink on court. You can't dig deeply into your opponent's mind. But you can get a good idea of how a player handles pressure just by catching a glimpse of an expression, a gesture or the way he walks around between points.

Reading an opponent's attitude is not something you start out doing early in a match. At that time, every player is eager and fired up. He feels good and he's not tired. But the longer the match lasts and the tougher the situations get, the more likely an opponent is to reveal his inner thoughts by arguing with linespeople, talking to himself or just shrugging his shoulders.

In the last 15 years, I've learned a lot by watching opponents and how they handle pressure. And that knowledge has paid off in a number of big matches. It can for you, too.

You're rarely going to face an opponent who always wears a blank, emotionless face like Bjorn Borg (above). Holding that much emotion and pressure inside is extremely difficult to do, especially at the club level. Against such a cool opponent, though, you've got your work cut out for you. You just have to try to keep grinding away.

Players who show frustration and fatigue, however, are much more common and they're often easier to handle. Attack them the same way you do emotionless players by keeping on top of them and not letting them get back into the flow of the match. The difference, though, is to direct your attack to the specific weaknesses that are causing their problems.

For example, if you find that something bothers an opponent, whether it's a certain shot pattern or type of spin, keep throwing it in there. And when an opponent shows signs of fatigue, don't let up. Move him around the court until he folds.

Of course, even the most accurate reading of an opponent's mental condition isn't going to guarantee that you'll win a particular match. So don't go on court with that idea. Just consider yourself lucky if you happen to see a gesture or expression during play that helps you out in your attack. But always stay on guard. The flow of a tennis match can change from one shot to the next.

concerns. But when the chair umpire says, "Play!" the opposite is true. I can change gears instantly and tennis becomes kind of a therapy for me, helping me put aside all outside distractions. From the moment the first ball is hit in a match, all of my efforts are focused on getting the job done on court.

That's not to say I'm thinking strategy every second in a match. That type of mental strain can be very exhausting. I think that proper relaxation is a vital factor in helping you to concentrate over the entire time span of a match—whether it's a quick, 45-minute match or a five-set marathon complete with tiebreakers.

The time for relaxation is between points and on changeovers. Through the years, I've learned how to use the 30-second clock between points. If I need to regain my composure after a tough point or a bad line call, I'll take 29 seconds.

And what I'm doing during that time is not worrying about the next point or game or how a call might turn around the match. Instead, I try to distract myself and divert my thoughts from the pressures of the situation. In other words, I let my mind wander. I might look into the crowd to see if my kids and Patti are there or to spot the television cameras. I'll stroll back to the fence to towel off the grip, I'll dust the line with my shoe, I'll play with my strings. All I'm doing is putting my mind at ease so that once I look up to begin the next point, I'm prepared to play, ready to grind things out with as fresh a mental attitude as possible.

While relaxation is important, you've got to play with some level of tension. The trick is to keep the tension manageable.

That level varies from player to player. So it's important to know your own game and personality in order to let the tension work for you, keeping you sharp and alert, rather than let it pull down your game. I actually look forward to tight squeezes now in matches because the way I relax on court prepares me for whatever is to come.

I've found that another way to keep mentally sharp on court is to avoid storing up anger or frustration. My anger and emotions in a match are always directed at myself to get me going. But I don't hold it inside. I try to let it all out at once and get rid of it so that I can concentrate on the next situation. The few times my anger has cost me a match have been when I spit out my anger just a little at a time during the course of an entire match. Each time, I let it prey on my mind and it affected my play.

Interacting with tennis crowds is one more way I try to use my emotional energy on court. It's a tremendous high to be playing a match, giving all you've got and hearing that the crowd is behind you. It just keeps you going and going. And I'll admit I like to fuel their fire through my gestures and expressions. I've done it all my life. I've always enjoyed performing for people. I appreciate them coming out to see me play.

What should you do when nothing seems to be working in a match?

The mark of a true champion, they say, is his ability to win matches even when he isn't playing his best. Nothing ever runs perfectly, so you shouldn't expect to play flawless tennis. That's why maintaining your mental composure under pressure is so important. Instead of getting down on yourself and going off the deep end when things go wrong, you should try to take a positive approach and maybe rearrange your tactics a little to compensate on an off-day.

Above all, always play within your ability. Play your own game. That way, you'll stay relaxed and mentally sharp. Remember, winning, at least 95 percent of it, is all in your mind!

HOW TO USE YOUR EMOTIONS TO WIN

Emotions. They're always intangible factors in the outcome of a tennis match. Properly controlled and channeled, they can keep your head above water in even the toughest of competitive situations. But let them run wild and they can be like lead weights strapped to your ankles, dragging you under to drown in defeat.

Consider my game, for example. Some people might look at the way I clench my fists, pump my arms, arch my back and yell at myself when I'm fired up and say that I'm crazy, that I've lost emotional control of myself. On the contrary, that's usually when I play my best.

And others, particularly my opponents, claim that my emotional displays on court are a form of gamesmanship. Of course, I can't argue with the fact that my gestures when I'm pumped up can have an unsettling effect on some players. I wear my emotions, especially the good ones, on my sleeve in a tight match. I like to show my excitement and the crowds seem to enjoy it as well. So when I play my heart out and the fans get behind me, I receive a big psychological lift and they get something extra, too.

But all my gestures are part of my natural way of expressing myself. I play the game hard-nosed, with the instincts of a street fighter, and my gestures represent my feelings. They're emotional responses that are automatically triggered at key points. Sometimes they come out in the wrong way . . . but nobody's perfect. I take full responsibility for both the good and the bad.

As for my opponents, I don't let what they do on their side of the court bother me, so what I do on my side shouldn't bother them.

I thrive on emotions. They're reflected in my game with aggressive play, with going forward all the time instead of holding back on shots, and with a heightened awareness of what's going on around me that I'd compare to an animal's instinct in hunting down its prey. My reactions on court are spontaneous reactions to high-pressure match situations that release emotional energy and allow me to raise my level of play a notch or two higher than before.

The way I look at it, a player's ability to use his emotions to his benefit, to channel all of that extra energy so it will boost the quality and intensity of his play, is a major key to his success in pro tennis. Without that type of

A winning edge: I thrive on emotions (right). They often boost my quality of play.

Consider your personality to get the most mileage from your emotions.

control, his future will always be limited. I think the same thing holds true for club players like you.

Now before you run off to the court and start practicing your Jimmy Connors clenched-fists, arched-back routine, I've got to warn you that my technique for dealing with my emotions and getting psyched up may not work for you. Besides that, you're not likely to win many popularity contests at your club by flashing your fists at an opponent.

What's most important in learning to channel your emotional energy in a positive way on court is to take your personality into consideration. In other words, take a long, hard look at yourself and what makes you tick. Do you enjoy confronting pressure situations head on with aggressive play? Or do you tend to back down a level in aggressiveness and concentrate on keeping ball after ball in play?

Once you've answered questions like that, you have to determine objectively whether those approaches have worked for you in the past. For example, if you pull out all the stops and play aggressively, but can't keep the ball in play because you're so hyper, you'd better experiment with a different type of emotional response in critical playing situations. The same is true if you tend to get despondent in tough situations and let your opponent run all over you.

So your personality characteristics are important in forming a game plan that will help you get the most mileage from your emotions. Can you imagine Bjorn Borg or Chris Evert Lloyd gesturing like I do and yelling, "C'mon, let's go!" after hitting a great shot? Their personalities wouldn't allow it.

And it's not that Bjorn and Chrissie play without emotion during a match. It's that they've learned that they function best when they conceal their feelings behind expressionless faces. Their way, I assure you, can have just as profound an effect on opponents, who wonder how they can keep so cool under intense match pressure.

Similarly, I couldn't handle my emotions the same way they do. I really believe that if I had kept all of my emotions locked up inside my head during my matches through the years, I probably would have been knocked out of the game long ago. I just can't let my emotions churn on the inside like that and expect to play my best.

In fact, I've paid a heavy price the few times that I have held back my emotions during my career. The match that immediately pops into my mind was a quarterfinal meeting with Argentina's Jose Luis Clerc in the 1981 French Open. I vividly recall I was leading two sets to one and the score was tight nearing the end of the fourth when I let a controversial line call get to me.

Instead of releasing all my emotions out at once and regaining my composure, I let my feelings spurt out a little at a time the rest of the way. My emotions kept simmering inside of me and it hurt my performance badly. I never was able to recover, and lost 6-0 in the fifth.

The great lesson to be learned here is that you shouldn't try to pattern your emotional responses after someone else's. What works for the person you're imitating may not work for you.

One of the questions I'm often asked about my emotional style of play is whether or not I can turn my emotions on and off at will to get pumped up at key moments in a match. I wish I could say it's as easy as turning a faucet handle, but it's not true. If it were, you can bet I'd have it running at full pressure throughout a tough match.

Actually, it's impossible to play at a feverish emotional peak for long. Why? Your body would use up far too much energy to keep you at that high level. No one has the physical stamina to get fired up at 1-all in the first set and sustain that level of play. From personal experience, I can tell you that the adrenaline bursts you get in an exciting situation last for only a few points—perhaps a couple of games at best. So it's important to conserve energy for use in the later stages of a match.

For me, the adrenaline seems to flow right into place on the most important occasions, usually after I've come up with a great shot when my back's up against the wall in a match. I'm sure you've probably felt the same wave of satisfaction come down over you when everything—your footwork, your strokes, your placements—seems to click under pressure. You get a tremendous emotional lift.

But even a bad line call can give you a much-needed shot in the arm if you look at it in the proper light. For example, it's absolutely critical to avoid the feeling of frustration. You can't afford to hang your head. If you do, you're just digging the hole deeper for yourself.

Instead of being weighted down with frustration, you should look to channel the powerful emotion of anger in a positive way. When I get mad about a line call, I'll direct my anger to influence my play. I'll use it to lift my game. I'm angry, but I'm taking advantage of it. That attitude has won a lot of matches for me.

Whether I've just hit a great shot or become fired up after a bad call, my mind seems to go on automatic pilot as my emotions surge. If I'm really getting stoked, the extra energy pounds through my body and I'll even feel a little light-headed. It may sound corny, but it's truly an emotional high.

Once you reach that point in a match, it's important to guard against a letdown. You know what I mean if you've ever pulled out an exceptionally tight tiebreaker and then had to scramble like mad to get back into the flow of play for the first couple of games in the following set. You can only get two or three big bursts of adrenaline in a match, so you have to make them count.

I try to compensate for the inevitable drops in energy level by concentrating as hard as possible. I focus on the ball and attack with an intensity that helps keep me playing near my peak, instead of dropping back to my previous level of play. The idea is to sustain your momentum. The longer you're able to do that, the more likely your opponent will crack under the pressure.

You also must be practical enough to realize that you'll have days when it will be tough to control and channel your emotional energy effectively. Sometimes, tennis fans don't understand that. They can have unrealistic expectations of the pro players. All of us who walk out on court are human beings, not infallible stars. We have our private lives, our business lives, our family lives. And with those other commitments come a truckload of emotions that are hard to wipe off the slate entirely. It's not always possible to take everything that happens on court in a positive manner.

But you've got to try. So remember, don't clench your fists and arch your back after you win key points just because I occasionally do it. Find your own way of handling your emotions during a match.

It will take some soul searching and some experimentation in game situations to arrive at a formula that works for you. But the results will be worth it. You'll be more than able to keep your head above water when the pressure threatens to pull you under.

MICHAEL BRENT/TENNIS MAGAZINE

Quick release (above): I can't let my emotions churn on the inside and expect to play my best.

SLICE & KICK SERVES: VARY YOUR SERVICE WITH SPIN

Show me a player whose only serving weapon is a flat cannonball delivery and I'll show you a player who loses a lot of matches because of inconsistency.

I've never been intimidated by a big server because I generally know that if I can make a decent return to start a rally, he's probably going to be on shaky ground. At that point, I've got him right where I want him. He has to play my game.

Putting on my other hat and speaking from a server's standpoint, I feel fortunate that I've never had to depend on blasting hard, flat serves past my opponents to win matches. Sure, it would be nice to take a few easy points that way occasionally, especially now that I'm getting older. But spin serves, specifically slice and kick deliveries, make far more effective and reliable weapons. They're what I use most often to get points under way and set up my second shots.

How does hitting a slice or kick serve differ from hitting a flat serve?

The big difference is the way your racquet meets the ball. For a flat serve, the simplest to learn, your racquet face hits the ball squarely. All of the momentum you generate with your shoulder turn, leg push-off and arm swing is transferred directly to the ball on impact. The result is a serve in which the ball flies in a nearly straight direction across the net. There is little spin on the ball to affect its flight.

But spin, of course, is the key element in effective slice and kick serves. It causes the ball to curve as it travels through the air and bounce in a couple of different ways that can create problems for the receiver.

With a good slice serve, for example, there's a sideways spin on the ball that makes it curve toward the deuce corner if you're a righthander, and toward the ad corner if you're a lefty. On the bounce, the ball tends to stay low and swerve toward the sideline.

To hit a slice serve, you don't meet the back of the ball squarely with your racquet as you would to hit a flat serve. Instead, you should swing your racquet so that it comes around the outside of the ball a little bit. In other words, it should brush across the back of the ball with a sideways motion to impart the spin you want. For righthanders, the brushing motion is from left to right; for lefthanders, it's right to left.

For a kick serve, you also need to brush the back of the ball with your

Service with some spin (right):
Slice or kick serves can create lots of
problems for receivers.

103

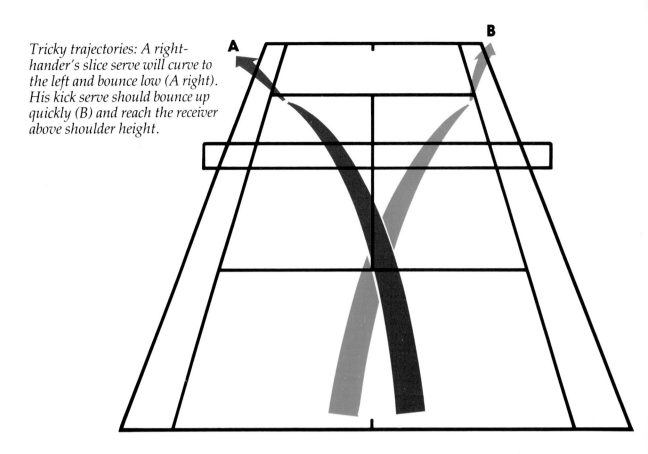

Tricky trajectories: A right-hander's slice serve will curve to the left and bounce low (A right). His kick serve should bounce up quickly (B) and reach the receiver above shoulder height.

racquet face, but at a different angle. Instead of coming across the ball with a sideways motion, you have to brush upward. That type of swing will produce what amounts to topspin, with a slight amount of sidespin as well.

The effect can be intimidating for an inexperienced receiver. Because you're brushing up on the ball, your kick serve won't carry as much speed as your flat serve, but it will kick up quickly on the bounce and stay high with a lot of spin as it reaches the baseline. If the receiver stays back, he's faced with the tough task of returning a ball above shoulder height. He won't be able to get much leverage into his shot.

Besides the added dimension of unusual bounces that spin serves give your game, they are also higher percentage deliveries. In each case, the extra spin you put on the ball helps it clear the net by a safer margin. So spin serves allow you to remain offensive minded and, at the same time, put a lot more first serves into play. That's a winning combination in my book.

You can make your spin serves even more effective if you can perfect a simple ball toss. I realize that the most widely accepted teaching wisdom tells you to toss the ball more out to your side for a slice serve and almost above your head for a kick serve. But if you can learn to hit both serves off the same toss, say one that's between those two points, you'll really keep your opponent guessing as he waits to return serve.

Throughout my career, I've always found that the pros who are able to disguise their serves the best with their tosses are the ones who'll give me the most trouble during their service games. Fortunately, most players do have slightly different tosses for their flat, slice and kick serves that provide

***S**pin serves allow you to remain offensive-minded and, at the same time, put a lot more first serves into play.*

me with clues about what type of delivery to expect.

I learned to use just one type of toss at a young age, mainly because I was too hard-headed to experiment a lot. In the long run, it has paid off. I may not blow a lot of first serves by my opponents, but they have to watch out for my spin and placements. My serves set up my second shots pretty well. Then, I'm off and running.

O.K., let's say you've mastered the stroking fundamentals of the three types of serves. Now, to be a server to be reckoned with, you've got to learn serving strategy—that is, when to use each serve and where to place it.

For some players, serving strategy means arriving at a specific plan even before a match starts. That way of thinking is counterproductive for me. If I went out to play and tried to stick to a plan, I'd be concerned that I would fall into a serving pattern that my opponent might figure out in a long match.

The key to my serving strategy has always been flexibility. I refuse to tie myself down to using specific serves in specific situations. I select my serve, whether it's a flat, hard one down the middle or a spinning kick into the corner, based on my instincts, what I feel is best at the time. I take things as they come and mix up my serves. That way, I don't feel locked into a serving strategy that's tough to break away from.

However, there are a few general guidelines I always keep in the back of my mind when I'm serving. They might help you as well. Here they are:

1. Against a slow player, try to break him wide of the court with a slice serve or a kicker to the backhand. If you can get him reaching to make a return, you should open up his court for your second shot.
2. A kick serve can be effective against a player who likes to return serve with a lot of topspin. If you're able to kick the ball up above his shoulders, especially on his backhand side, you'll probably force a weak slice or push return.
3. When you serve to a quick player, you should realize he's going to get to virtually every serve you hit. So instead of really cranking up and overhitting the ball, concentrate on moving the ball around with good placements. Also, a serve into the body occasionally may handcuff him on his return.
4. Don't overlook the advantage of serving down the middle. That placement will take away some of your opponent's return angles and will probably put you in good position to hit some solid ground strokes.

So learn to use spin serves along with your flat serves to create openings to attack with your following shots. And always expect a serve to be returned across the net. That way, you'll never be caught by surprise.

Even if you own a cannonball serve that's really hot, that attitude will bail you out of trouble more often than you think. Remember, aces don't win tennis matches. The biggest servers fall the hardest if they don't have the consistency to pull out matches when opponents are able to return their cannonballs with some firepower of their own.

KEYS TO SLICE AND KICK SERVES

THE SLICE SERVE

KEEP YOUR MOTION FLUID AND NATURAL

There isn't a more personal stroke in tennis than a serve. Every player, whether a pro or a beginner, puts his or her trademark on the serving motion right from the start. That's fine as long as the motion is fluid and natural.

I begin my natural rhythm for slice serves (see photo sequence above right) and kick serves (below right) by rocking back on my rear foot and dropping my ball-tossing arm at the same time (see photos 1 and 2). Next, I bring both arms up at the same time (3) in a continuation of the service motion.

THE KICK SERVE

TOSS THE BALL ACCURATELY

For the flat serve, an accurate ball toss helps ensure good timing and solid contact. The same is especially true for spin serves because the racquet face meets the ball with a brushing motion instead of hitting it straight on. Therefore, ball placement on the toss becomes even more important.

I've pretty much kept my toss the same for all of my serves, (4) in both photo sequences. In each case, my toss is out in front and just to the side of my body. As the ball is rising, I drop my racquet behind me (5 and 6) to cock it for the upward swing.

BRUSH THE BALL
TO IMPART SPIN

Up to this point in my serve, I haven't really given my opponent any clues as to what type of serve to expect. Now, as I begin to uncoil my upper body and start springing off the court with my legs, I'll swing my racquet up from my backscratching position (7 and 8) to meet the ball in one of two ways to impart spin.

For the slice serve, I'll meet the ball when I'm fully extended, brushing across the back of the ball with a sideways motion (8 and 9, above right). This stroking motion gives the ball side-spin.

For a kick serve, I'll try to make contact with the ball a little lower. That allows me to brush upward against the back of the ball to put topspin on it with only a slight amount of sidespin (8 and 9 below right).

8

9

8

9

FOLLOW THROUGH FOR GOOD PACE

A good follow-through is just as important on a spin serve as it is for a hard, flat serve. Many players think that because spin serves don't travel as fast as powerful deliveries, they need to slow down their swings.

That's a big mistake. I take a complete swing on my slice and kick serves, too. If I didn't, I wouldn't be able to put as much spin on the ball and my serves would be ineffective. The result is a full follow-through for both serves (right). The difference is that the upward brushing motion of the kick serve forces my racquet further out to the side of my body (10 and 11, below right) than for the slice serve above. In both cases, my racquet head continues smoothly through and beyond the contact zone with all of the momentum my body has generated (12).

THE APPROACH SHOT: HIT OUT AGGRESSIVELY

I have what you might call a healthy disrespect for tennis balls. I dislike them so much that whenever one lands short or just floats into my half of the court, I don't want to see it come back again during that point. So I'll move in at every opportunity, put my whole body into the approach shot and try to hit the ball so solidly that it's gone.

In that way, I go contrary to the accepted wisdom, which says that an approach shot should be more of a placement shot, not a winner, hit with underspin to keep the ball low to the court after the bounce.

I like to hit out on the ball firmly and solidly, just like I do on conventional ground strokes. I'll even go for quite a few winners off my approach. If I can make contact with a short ball above waist level, I'll usually drive it with little or no spin into an opening in my opponent's court. The ball is hit flat and with enough power to make it stay low to the court, too.

Of course, I will use slice approach shots in some situations. On low balls, for example, slice gives you more control to place the ball deep with accuracy. I could use it above waist level, too, but I feel that it takes too much sting out of my approach shots.

I'm not suggesting that you go out on court and start blasting all of your approach shots, aiming for the lines. My aggressive style of approaching the net works for me, but it probably won't for club players. Nevertheless, you can still hit effective approaches with good shot placement.

There are three stroking keys to help you do that and make your approaches tough to handle: proper concentration, a short backswing and hitting the ball on the rise.

Because weak returns can come across the net at any time during a point, you have to stay awake. Good concentration is the answer. When I'm playing my best, for example, I'm focusing on just one thing—the tennis ball.

Whether I'm playing John McEnroe, Ivan Lendl or Ilie Nastase, it doesn't matter. He's just a blur on the other side of the net. You have to

A sound approach: Hit your approach shot on the move (left) and follow it to the net. Don't wait to see how good your shot is going to be.

Picking off a floater: If you're alert enough, you should hit a floating ball before it bounces with a volleying-type motion (right).

learn to just play the ball and not worry about what your opponent is doing.

The second key to a good approach shot is a compact backswing. Although Borg and some other players are able to hit effective approaches with big looping backswings, it might help a lot of club players to cut down on their backswings. All of my strokes are compact and I think it helps in approaching the net. How? With a short backswing, you reduce your chances of mistiming your shot, especially if you misjudge the direction of your opponent's shot or a small gust of wind makes the ball jump unexpectedly.

Taking the ball early, on the rise, gives you another little edge in taking control of a point. I always try to meet the ball before it has reached its peak after bouncing. That way, I make contact above the level of the net and can hit the ball flat. If you can make taking the ball on the rise a habit, you'll also find yourself a step closer to the net when you decide to move in during a point. It keeps opponents off balance and wears them down because they always have to react quickly to your shots, not the other way around.

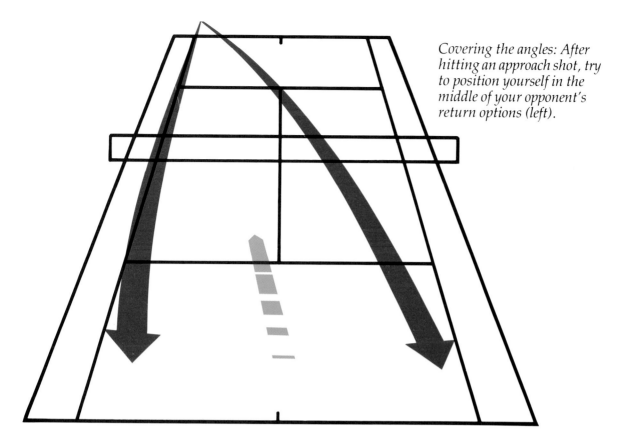

Covering the angles: After hitting an approach shot, try to position yourself in the middle of your opponent's return options (left).

Where should you aim your approach shots? It depends a lot on your ability and your opponent's weaknesses. But a general rule of thumb is to keep the ball in front of you when you go to the net. In other words, go down the line most often to cut down the possible angles of return. Your chances of success will increase, too, if you exploit an opponent's weak side.

Court surface is also a consideration in placing your approaches. On hard courts, I go crosscourt rather than down the line if my opponent is out of position. The combination of the fast surface and my shot's power will usually add up to an unreturnable ball. And on a soft, clay court, you shouldn't overlook an approach behind a player who is scrambling to get back into position. Once he gets his weight moving quickly in one direction, it's extremely difficult to change course abruptly.

One last piece of advice: Hit your approach shots on the move and follow them all the way in to the net. The one thing you don't want to do is hit the ball and stand there watching it, hoping it will be good. The whole objective behind moving in is to end points quickly, so you've got to close in on the net even if you mis-hit the ball. You never know; a rush of wind or a mis-hit could still put you in great shape at the net.

In golf, there's a saying about putting: "Never up, never in." It means that you've got to hit the ball hard enough so that it will reach the hole or it will never have a chance to drop. In a way, the same thought applies to moving up to the net in tennis. If you hit an approach shot and don't follow it in, you're going to watch a lot of passing shots fly by you.

To sum up my thoughts, try to avoid falling into a stroking rut at the baseline. Shake up your opponents by moving in aggressively whenever you get an opportunity.

And remember, don't retreat. Hit your approach shots with a purpose and never let up in your attack once you reach the net. It's a sure bet you'll earn a lot more respect from your opponents.

KEYS TO THE APPROACH SHOT

KEEP YOUR RACQUET PREPARATION SHORT

The sooner you're able to determine that an opponent's shot is going to land short in your court, the more time you'll have to move in with quick, sure footwork and set up for your approach.

Because one of the strengths of my ground game is taking balls on the rise, I usually get a quick jump on the ball. As I move into the court to hit an approach shot, I immediately start to take my racquet back and turn my upper body sideways to the net (see photo 1 below).

By the time I reach the area of the court where I'm going to make contact with the ball, my backswing is complete. As you can see, I keep my racquet preparation short and sweet (2 and 3) to increase my chances of timing the hit perfectly.

HIT THE BALL WITH A CONTROLLED STROKE

If your footwork is good, you should never have to hit an approach shot on the dead run. Instead, you should have your forward momentum under full control as you make your stroke.

At the point I start my forward swing (4), I've committed myself to a specific placement. There's no time to change my mind at this point. I hit the ball with a smooth, flat stroke (5 and 6), aiming for a spot that's deep near my opponent's baseline.

When you hit an approach off a lower ball, be sure to bend at the knees and waist and swing from high to low to put underspin on your shot. That type of stroke will help the ball clear the net safely and place it deep, where it will bounce low because of its spin.

6

FINISH WITH A COMPLETE FOLLOW-THROUGH

I think one of the biggest mistakes you can make when hitting an approach shot is stroking the ball tentatively. If you hold back on your stroke to make sure the ball stays in play, your approach is liable to be very weak. You can also expect to see a winning passing shot fly past you.

To ensure that doesn't happen, you should finish your stroke with a complete follow-through, as I'm demonstrating in photos 7 through 9. It's a checkpoint that indicates you've used a smooth, steady stroke. Your follow-through should also open your shoulders automatically toward the net. With your momentum still carrying you forward, you should be able to move to the net easily behind your approach and set up for a solid volley.

9

THE OFFENSIVE LOB:
SURPRISE
THE NET-HUGGER

The word "intimidation" has almost taken on a new meaning in recent years with the evolution of a more aggressive, all-court style of tennis. Gone are the days when the game was dominated by baseline specialists like Bjorn Borg or Guillermo Vilas. Their tremendous influence, which reached all the way to the club level, has been replaced with a daring, offensive-minded approach.

Today, more and more players are frequently advancing to the net and taking up an intimidating volleying position just a few feet from the net. From there, they practically dare you to hit a passing shot by them. When you do, you often try to go for too much with your shot, firing it long or into the net.

How can you beat these net-huggers . . . or at least make them think twice about crowding the net so closely?

Develop a good offensive lob. I don't think there's another shot that can top the offensive lob for stopping net-rushers dead in their tracks and forcing them to turn tail to run down the ball. I can tell you it's really satisfying and a lot of fun to watch the expressions of confidence on their faces turn into surprise and sometimes panic when they catch sight of a shot they know will be too high to reach from their net position.

The offensive lob has been a part of my game for years and years. In fact, I was hitting good, effective offensive lobs in junior matches long before I ever felt comfortable with the defensive lob (see Chapter 7) in college. That's because my ground strokes and passing shots set up the shot. My opponents usually were so concerned with stopping my ground game that the possibility I might lift the ball over their heads and into the backcourt rarely entered their minds.

Having that element of variety in my game is even more important now because today's players are bigger, stronger and smarter than ever before. So I like to give them as much to think about as I can when they're on their way to the net. Every doubt I can plant in their minds as to what shot I'm going to try next works in my favor.

Offensive lobs are natural, spur-of-the-moment shots for me. I think of them as aces I keep up my sleeve in a match. I'm not going to string together four or five offensive lobs in successive points, or even games, since I don't want my opponent to learn to anticipate them. They're most effective when used sparingly and in the right situations.

For me, those situations occur when an opponent has hit an approach

Keeping a volleyer honest: An offensive lob (left) can force the net-hugger to retreat.

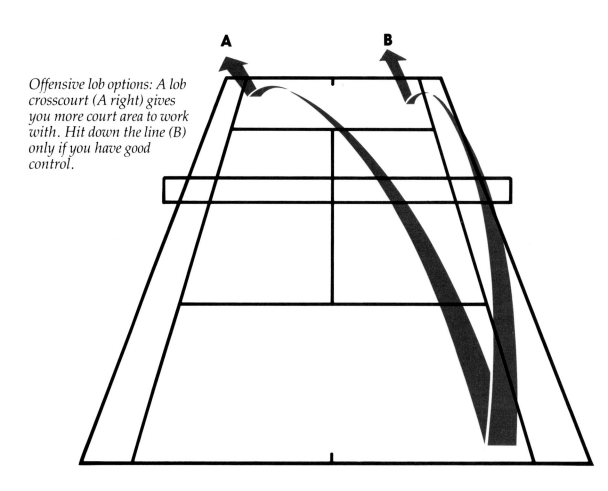

Offensive lob options: A lob crosscourt (A right) gives you more court area to work with. Hit down the line (B) only if you have good control.

shot or volley that I'm able to reach comfortably, either near or inside the baseline. Normally, I'll go for my bread-and-butter stroke, the passing shot, but if he's been jamming the net a lot, I'll try to catch him leaning forward.

How? By disguising my swing and holding back on the shot until my opponent has committed himself to move one way or another.

The surest way to hide your intentions is to take a normal ground stroke backswing. Then, instead of driving through the ball on the forward stroke, use your racquet to brush upward on the ball and send it arcing skyward quickly with a moderate amount of topspin.

I'm sure you've seen other pros hit their offensive lobs with a lot of topspin. Ivan Lendl and Ilie Nastase, for example, use a quick wrist snap at impact with the ball to send it spinning over an opponent's head. That technique is fine if you have strong wrists and a fine sense of timing to meet the ball cleanly at impact.

However, I always boil down strokes to their simplest common denominator. That is, I keep everything as uncomplicated as possible to reduce the number of mistakes that I could make. With an extreme topspin offensive lob, you always run the risk of mistiming the hit and, worse still, of brushing upward on the ball so sharply that it takes its nosedive out of the air too early. With a more moderate amount of topspin, your low-to-high swing is more controlled and you can use a smooth follow-through to place the ball deep and with accuracy into your opponent's backcourt.

The target area I pick for an offensive lob often depends on whether I've hit the ball off my forehand or backhand side. Off the forehand, I'll usually place the ball crosscourt because doing that will give me a lot of court to hit into.

I'm more confident when hitting a backhand offensive lob, though. My

I *think of offensive lobs as aces I keep up my sleeve in a match. They're most effective when used sparingly.*

two-handed grip gives me more control of the shot, so I'm able to hold the racquet head back until the very last second, forcing my opponent to commit himself. Off the backhand side, I can go down the line or crosscourt.

I think one of the best percentage placements for the offensive lob is over the netman's backhand side. That way, even if the lob comes down a little short, he'll have to hit the ball with a backhand overhead, a tough shot to put away even among the pros.

After you send the ball on its way, you should stay alert to move to the net and pick off your opponent's return. If you're not experienced enough to know how good your lob will be as soon as it leaves your strings, just take a look at your opponent's reaction. He'll spin around and take off after the ball like crazy if it's a good lob. That's your cue to advance to the forecourt and wait for what's likely to be a weak return or defensive lob.

So remember, don't let an over-aggressive opponent intimidate you. Use the offensive lob wisely and you'll be the one who does the intimidating. He'll keep a respectful distance from the net.

Gaining a breather: If you need to catch your breath in a point and your opponent is staying back, throw up a high looper from the backcourt (right) with your offensive-lob hitting motion.

KEYS TO THE OFFENSIVE LOB

DISGUISE YOUR BACKSWING

An offensive lob is a great weapon to have in your game if you're facing an opponent who likes to hang his head over the net. But you have to resist the temptation to go to the well too often.

You should use the offensive lob sparingly and only when you're in good position, either near or inside the baseline (see photos 1 and 2). That way, you'll have time to set up properly for the shot and make a smooth, controlled stroke.

To prepare, take your racquet back the same way you would to hit a topspin ground stroke as I'm demonstrating below, with your racquet head finishing slightly below the point where you expect to make contact with the ball (3).

3

LIFT THE BALL AND LOOK TO MOVE IN

From your relatively low starting point, swing your racquet head forward and up (4) so that it meets the ball a little above waist level and in front of your body (5). That low-to-high swing allows me to put a modest amount of topspin on the ball which will help bring it down into my opponent's backcourt.

Your follow-through (6 and 7) should be a smooth, natural extension of your forward swing for an accurate placement.

If you've fooled your opponent, he's going to be scrambling like mad to run down your lob. So you should be prepared to move in behind your shot.

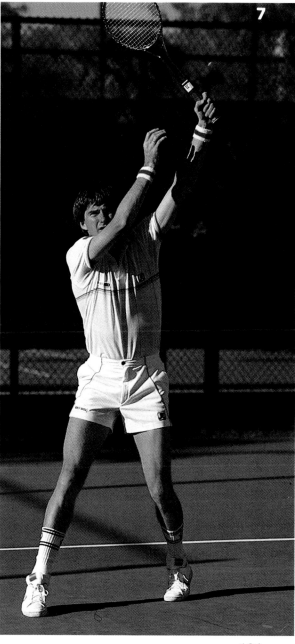

THE HALF VOLLEY:
HANG IN THERE FOR SOLID CONTACT

Ask any of your friends who play tennis which shot they find toughest to hit and they're almost sure to tell you it's the half volley. It's not the backhand overhead, the twist serve or even the reflex volley of a powerful drive that's headed straight for the mid-section. No, the half volley usually wins this lack-of-popularity contest hands down.

I'd be willing to bet that you'd cast your vote in favor of the half volley as well. More often than you'd probably like to admit, you've felt that unwelcome wave of anxiety surge inside you when an opponent is able to pound a tough return right at your feet. In fact, the strength of his return may catch you so much by surprise that it almost knocks you backward. You've pushed the panic button and it shows in your timid reaction to the return.

Now, I'm not going to tell you that the half volley is an easy shot to hit. It certainly isn't. If given a choice, I'd prefer not to have to hit another half volley the rest of my life. I think most of my fellow pros would side with me on that—even a player like John McEnroe who is occasionally able to hit clean winners with the shot.

However, it is important that you learn to hang in there when an opponent hits a sizzling drive at your feet and react with confidence to get the ball back across the net, with something on it, you hope. I've even learned that the half volley can be an offensive weapon in my game when I use it properly from the baseline. If you can make similar adjustments in your attitude, you won't have to hit the panic button often in your matches.

Whenever I'm forced to hit a half volley from no-man's land, I know it's because I came in behind a weak serve or approach shot, I got lazy on my footwork or my opponent hit a great return. In the last case, I've learned to give credit where credit is due and move on to play the next point. But if the half-volley situation is the result of one of the first two problems, then I realize I have to go back and really concentrate on the shot I hit poorly.

Technically, the stroke is short and sweet. There's nothing fancy about the half volley because timing is critical. Your job is to block back a return that bounces at your feet a split-second after it hits the court surface. Otherwise, the ball will get by you. In effect, the half volley represents an extreme case of having to hit the ball on the rise. You have to make contact a

Solid technique: Imagine that your racquet is a wall.
Keep a firm grip (right) and block the ball back deep.

With a solid half volley, you'll challenge your opponent to string together a few fine shots to put the point on ice.

lot earlier than you would to hit a normal ground stroke return.

To get that job done right, you should set two main priorities for yourself. First, you need to keep your weight forward. If you flinch when you see you're going to have to hit a half volley, your body weight will tend to fall backward at impact and that will virtually eliminate any chance you have of hitting an effective return.

Second, you've got to get your racquet and your body down low to the court surface to help guarantee solid contact. That's where most players make their biggest mistake on the half volley. They stand up too straight, partly as the result of being surprised by the strong return, and have to use a big arm swing to meet the ball. Of course, there isn't a chance in the world that they can get any kind of accuracy with such a stroke.

Another common problem occurs when you lower your body for the shot, but leave your racquet head too high on the backswing. In this case, a level or high-to-low swing is the result. Both are likely to send the ball into the net. If these symptoms sound familiar, then I'd suggest you exaggerate getting your racquet head down low in practice sessions by actually touching the court surface before you start your forward stroke. You'll soon see your half volleys clearing the net by a safer margin.

The stroke itself is a simple one, as you can see in the photo sequence on the next few pages. I keep my backswing short so I'm able to time the hit more precisely. From that starting position, I move the racquet forward with a firm grip and block the ball solidly out in front of my body, immediately after it hits the court. The sounds of the ball bouncing off the court and then my strings should be separated by only a split-second of time.

You might have an easier time with the short stroke if you think of your racquet as a solid wall. I remember when I was a kid that we used to throw balls so they'd bounce off the ground just a few inches in front of a brick wall. The balls would bounce up quickly and hit the wall, rebounding back to us with a surprising amount of pace. That's exactly the type of solid blocking motion you're after. So keep your stroke short and your grip firm.

My follow-through, like my backswing, is relatively short, too. That's because I don't have to supply much power on the shot. I use the pace of my opponent's return and my blocking-type stroke to send the ball back across the net.

In placing the ball, I think mainly of getting good depth on my half volley so my opponent isn't able to move in with a lot of confidence and hit an aggressive return. If I have enough time to set up for the shot, of course, I'll try to place it on his weaker side. But that's often a luxury in half-volley situations. Many times, you're lucky just to get the ball back in play.

After you hit a half volley, you should make it a point to move in toward the net quickly. Why? If your ball's short and you hold your ground near the service line or begin to back up, your opponent will be able to beat you easily. At the net, though, you'll at least force him to come up with a pretty good passing shot.

While hitting a half volley from the vicinity of the service line usually leaves you in a defensive position, hitting one from the baseline can put you in good shape during a point. Not too many players exploit the shot's potential from the backcourt, but I use it more often there. The tactic has

An unusual tactic: Hitting a half volley from the baseline (left) is an aggressive move because you've chosen to take the ball on the rise.

paid off for me many times in my career.

Here's the way it usually works. My opponent and I are in the middle of a rally in which we're moving each other around, trying to gain an advantage in positioning. He hits a good, deep ground stroke and he thinks he's got me trapped way behind the baseline. But instead of backing up to hit the ball at comfortable waist level, I'll sometimes take a step or two into the court and hit a half volley.

My rationale for that aggressive move is to turn the tables on my opponent. If I can meet the ball early after the bounce and place it deep into a corner away from him, I'll have him on the run. He won't have much time to recover from his deep return and track down my shot.

Like the half volley hit from inside the court, the half volley from the baseline is a short stroke, but the follow-through is a little longer because you have to send the ball the full length of the court. A firm grip is another stroking essential.

Try hitting a few offensive half volleys from your baseline the next time you play. Be sure to hold your ground, though. You might be able to sneak in to the net behind the shot now and then. Once you see that you're able to push your opponent around with the half volley from the baseline, you'll probably gain valuable confidence when it comes time to hit one from the service-line area of your court.

You probably still won't like to make the shot from that close to the net, but at least you won't be falling back on your heels. You'll challenge your opponent to string together two or three fine shots to put the point on ice. If he's able to pull off that feat, he deserves the point. You'll have done your best with the half volley and that's all anyone can ask.

KEYS TO THE HALF VOLLEY

BEND TO GET LOW TO THE COURT

Although there are a lot more powerful shots in tennis that you must deal with, probably the most intimidating one is a tough return hit right at your feet.

In this photo sequence, you can see that my body weight is forward when I prepare for the half volley. Although I'm caught by surprise by my opponent's return, I make sure I don't fall back on my heels.

Because timing is critical in hitting a half volley, you have to keep your preparation compact. The simpler the better. In photos 1 and 2, notice that I'm bending at my knees and waist to get low to the court at the same time I'm bringing my racquet back. Both movements have to be done in unison or I won't have time to prepare.

My backswing is short and low (3) because I have to hit the ball on the rise, immediately after it bounces off the court. Good timing is extremely important, so any extra racquet movement can be disastrous.

BLOCK THE BALL SOLIDLY LIKE A WALL

You should think of your racquet as a wall on the half volley. That thought should help you keep your stroke short and increase your chances of making solid contact.

From my racquet's low starting point, I move the racquet head forward and upward slightly to make contact with the ball out in front of my body, if possible (4). My grip is firm at contact and that's what gives me a solid blocking effect like a wall.

If you keep your forward stroke short, you won't have to worry about your follow-through because your racquet head will have little forward movement.

In photos 5 through 7, you'll notice that my follow-through on the half volley is compact. Its only real purpose is to finish off the stroke and help guide the ball to the target I've selected—deep and to my opponent's weaker side, if possible. Hopefully, if my half volley is good enough, I'm back in the thick of things.

THE OUTSIDE-IN GROUND STROKE: THROW OPPONENTS THE CURVE

I n baseball, a young pitcher can jump quickly into the major leagues if he's got a blazing fastball that he can throw past the best batters. Often, that successful strikeout pitch can be enough to carry him to stardom during the first few years of his career.

But as he grows more experienced, the smart pitcher will learn to add another pitch to his game, perhaps a curveball or a change of pace, that makes it considerably more difficult for opposing batters to find their timing at the plate. They can't sit back and wait for the fastball every time. In effect, the off-speed pitch makes his fastball even tougher to hit.

In a way, I'm a lot like a baseball pitcher out on the tennis court. My strikeout pitch, the one I've always relied on, is a powerful ground stroke that lands deep in my opponent's court. And my curveball is what I like to call an outside-in ground stroke.

What is it? My outside-in ground stroke is a shot I usually hit from the center of the court and a step or two inside the baseline. It appears at first to travel on a straight line, but then curves out into one of the corners of the court. It's a medium-paced ball that I'll throw in during rallies to keep an opponent honest. It effectively mixes up the pace of my ground strokes.

It's not a stroke that gets a lot of attention, especially from fans, because there's not a lot of flair involved. Unlike my skyhook overhead, for example, which demands a lot of physical effort that's easy to spot from the stands, my outside-in ground strokes are not spectacular. I don't need to use as much effort to hit the ball and the shots don't often fall for clean winners. So although I've been using the shot more often than ever during the past few years, you may not have even noticed it.

A change of pace: Control is needed to place the outside-in ground stroke (left) effectively.

Control is the name of the game with the stroke because it's an off-speed type of shot.

Both the forehand and backhand outside-in ground strokes came naturally to me when I was a junior. I was never taught to hit the shots. I guess they're the results of my own creativity on court, the same type of experimentation that produces distinctive elements in every player's stroking style.

Of course, I don't claim to be the only player who uses the outside-in shot. Many players do, including Chris Evert Lloyd, who hits the shot during baseline rallies at times to move her opponents around more effectively. And I think it's the type of stroke that would easily fit into most club players' games, too.

In order to hit an outside-in ground stroke, you need to keep your backswing short. That's never been a problem for me because my whole stroking style is based on compact swings. If your normal backswing is a long and complicated one, you might have a little trouble controlling this shot.

Control is really the name of the game with the stroke because it's an off-speed type of shot. You're not trying to blast the ball past your opponent. If that's your objective in a certain playing situation, then there are a few other more suitable weapons you should consider using.

The path of your racquet head during the forward swing through the contact zone is from outside to inside. That's what gives the stroke its name. With such a swing, the racquet strings brush across the back of the ball, imparting sidespin. I find that I can control the brushing motion more effectively if I make contact farther out in front of my body than I would for a normal ground stroke.

When you attempt an outside-in shot, you should be careful not to take too much pace off the ball by slowing down your swing or trying to hit it with a lot of underspin. True, the shot is an off-speed one, but its reduced pace is the result of the brushing motion of your swing.

A complete follow-through serves as an indication that you've finished the stroke properly. For example, I can tell that I've hit the ball well when my racquet head finishes well out in front of my body, but more to the inside, than on a conventional follow-through. You can use your follow-through as a checkpoint, too.

The path of the ball after it leaves your racquet is just the reverse of your outside-in swing. It will travel inside-out from the center of the court toward a corner (see next page). The curving motion is the result of the sidespin you've imparted to the ball with your stroke. You should always take this motion into consideration when you hit the ball. Aim for a target along the baseline that's a few feet from the corner where you want the ball to land in order to compensate for its curving flight.

After the bounce, the ball tends to stay low and pull your opponent into the alley. One of my favorite plays with the shot off my forehand side is to send the ball deep into the deuce corner and away from a right-hander's forehand. The outside-in shot forces him into the alley and opens up a lot of the court for my next return. If he's scrambling hard in anticipation of a crosscourt return, I like to fire a backhand down the line behind him. That's a good percentage shot for me. But if he stays, the crosscourt opening is a huge target that's tough to miss.

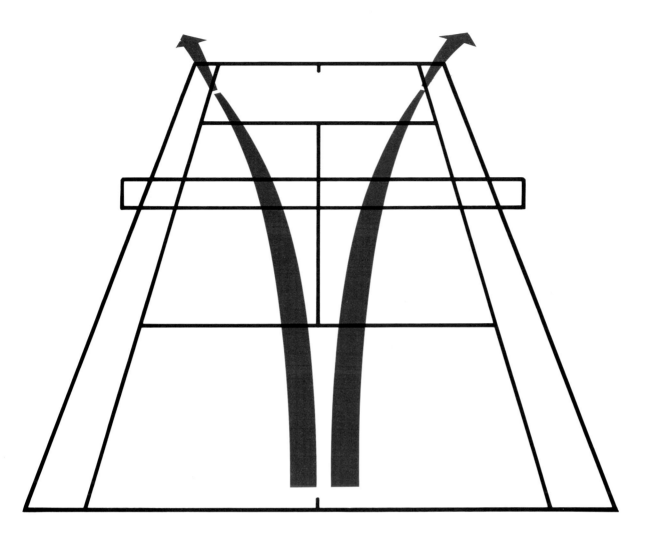

Playing the curve: Be sure to take the curving trajectories of outside-in ground strokes into consideration when placing the ball. The shots will curve toward the corners (above).

As you might guess, the outside-in return can be used effectively as an approach shot, as well as an off-pace shot to disrupt an opponent's rhythm. In fact, I'll often try to sneak in behind one of these shots if I can see that my opponent will have a tough time making a strong return. I suggest you try the same tactic in your matches. You'll probably catch a lot of players by surprise.

That's the lowdown on the outside-in return. It's not a spectacular shot, but it can be a valuable tool to have at your disposal during the course of a match. It's a relatively risk-free, high-percentage shot because you're not hitting out to catch a line. At the same time, you're working the ball and your opponent with a definite purpose in mind. That virtually guarantees you'll raise the level of your game. If you're a smart player, how can you turn down that kind of deal?

KEYS TO THE OUTSIDE-IN GROUND STROKE

GET SET NEAR THE MIDDLE OF THE BASELINE
Positioning is a major key to hitting an effective outside-in ground stroke. I like to hit the shot off an opponent's return that I can meet in the middle of the court, a step or two inside the baseline (see photo 1 below).

Because it's not an attacking shot, I have to be pretty well set with my feet when I begin the stroke (2). If I ran through the shot or met the ball while it was on the rise, I'd lose a lot of control. A compact backswing minimizes the chances of mistiming your hit (3).

3

4

146   OUTSIDE-IN GROUND STROKE

BRUSH ACROSS THE BACK OF THE BALL

My forward stroke through the contact zone is an outside-in motion that allows the racquet head to brush across the back of the ball and impart sidespin (4). If I'm able to meet the ball at a comfortable height, I'll also swing slightly from high to low to add some underspin to the ball as well. Because the outside-in ground stroke should travel the length of the court and land deep near your opponent's baseline, you must be sure to complete your follow-through. It differs from a regular ground stoke follow-through in that your racquet should finish well out in front but more to the inside of your body, as I'm demonstrating in photos 5 and 6.

THE DROP SHOT: CATCH THE OPPOSITION FLAT-FOOTED

Put yourself in my opponent's shoes for just a minute. We're in the middle of a tough match and I've consistently kept you pinned behind your baseline with good pace on my ground strokes. What's the shot you'd least expect from me during a rally?

Right, a drop shot. The chances are that you'd be so surprised at my shot selection that you might not be able to get your feet moving in time to reach the ball. But even if you did, you'd most likely be so stretched out and on a dead run that you wouldn't be able to manage much of a return.

Now, I don't hit many drop shots in a match. In fact, you may not see me hit one for a couple of matches at a time. But that's the key to the effectiveness of my drop shot. I don't pretend to have the great touch of a John McEnroe, a Chris Evert Lloyd or an Ilie Nastase. I rely more on picking the right time to try the drop shot so that it doesn't have to be hit perfectly. That approach has worked nicely for me.

I think many club players place far too much importance on this difficult shot. You've probably felt like kicking yourself many times in your matches for attempting to drop the ball across the net in situations that demand a near–impossible placement. In a fast-paced rally, it's easy to forget that the drop shot is a risky, low-percentage choice.

I consider myself fortunate that I've learned to increase my chances of success with the shot by using it sparingly, only when I'm in control of the flow of a point. So let me share some of my thoughts on the drop shot with you. Perhaps you'll come to the same conclusion.

One of the most important elements a drop shot attempt must have going for it is disguise. In other words, you've got to make your opponent think he's about to see another ground stroke return during a rally. One of the ways you can do that is to condition your opponent to a particular rhythm or pattern of shots.

That job is fairly easy for me because of the nature of my game. My opponent sees so many deep ground strokes that he's always anticipating another. When I'm ahead in a game, say 30-0 or 40-15, and I'm at least a step or two inside the baseline, I have enough confidence in my drop shot to slip one in and catch him napping. If he's completely surprised and out of position, then my drop shot doesn't have to be hit perfectly to be

An offensive tool: I'll sometimes use the
drop shot (left) to set up a point.

I *increase my chances of success with the shot by using it sparingly, only when I'm in control of the flow of a point.*

effective. I usually have a little larger margin for error to work with in terms of placement.

In fact, I'll frequently go for what is generally considered the lowest-percentage drop shot by hitting the ball over the highest part of the net and down the line. The reason I can get away with doing that is because my drop shot attempt will often follow a crosscourt backhand I've driven deep into the deuce corner. In that situation, my backhand opens up the whole ad side of my opponent's court to hit into. The empty court is an invitation I can't resist.

Besides conditioning your opponent to expect another deep ground stroke, you have to disguise your drop shot from a technical standpoint. The key is your backswing. You must take your racquet back so that it is higher than the spot where you plan to make contact with the ball. From the other side of the net, your backswing should look the same as one you'd take to hit a slice ground stroke (see the photo sequence that follows).

Then, you swing forward and slightly downward in a smooth motion, relaxing your grip and opening your racquet face a little at contact . . . just enough to take the pace off your opponent's shot. The ball should leave your racquet face softly and with a little underspin so that it dies in the forecourt after it has cleared the net.

I don't mean to make the stroke sound easy because it really isn't. The drop shot requires a delicate touch that many power players don't possess. That's why I'll pick the times to use it carefully. Nine times out of 10 when a short ball lands in my court, I'll quickly move inside the baseline, drive the ball deep into a corner and follow the shot to the net. When I do decide to try a drop shot, it's usually off my backhand side because my two-handed grip gives me a little more control of my racquet head.

Another reason why I've had some success with the shot is because I've never considered it a point winner. In other words, I've never hit a drop shot and said to myself, "That's the point. I've got it."

That's the trap that many players fall into. They hit the drop shot and stand there watching their opponents scramble for the ball. They don't prepare for a return and often get caught by surprise as a result.

I consider the drop shot just another tool to set up a point. It's not a magical point winner when it comes off my racquet. In fact, because I'm not a great touch player, I always assume that my opponent will reach the ball. So once I hit the ball, I stay alert.

I have two basic options at this point. First, I can move in close to the net, anticipating a weak, floating return that I can pick off in mid-air before the ball bounces. That's the strategy used by a lot of the pro players.

The second choice, and the one I rely on most often, is to play three-quarter court and stay on my toes to finish off the point. I have enough experience to know how good my drop shot is going to be as soon as the ball leaves my strings. For that reason, I don't believe staying put in no-man's land is terribly risky.

If I know that my shot is good enough to force my opponent to stretch out, I'm in a good position to move in any direction quite comfortably, forward or sideways, to make a strong return that will probably end the point.

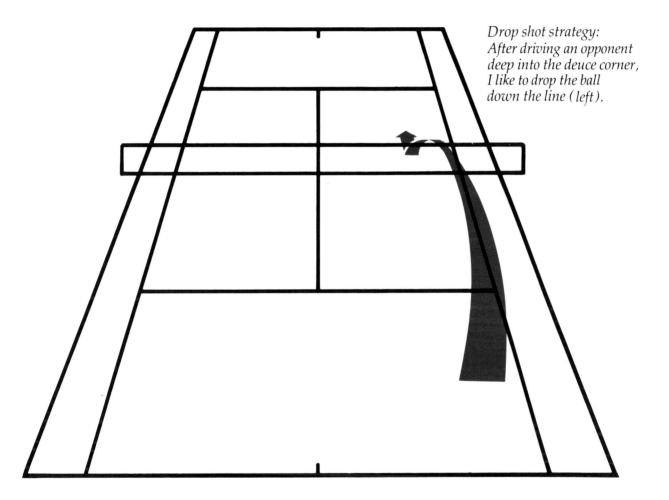

Drop shot strategy: After driving an opponent deep into the deuce corner, I like to drop the ball down the line (left).

Good anticipation of my opponent's likely return also gives me an edge from my three-quarter-court position. For example, if I place my drop shot over the net and down the line, I can usually be sure that my opponent will try to return the ball crosscourt.

Why? If he's really stretched out, a return down the line would have to be hit upward to clear the net. The ball would tend to float and might become an easy sitter. By going crosscourt, he can angle the ball over the middle, or lowest, part of the net. That's the shot I'd be looking for.

Should you add a drop shot to your game? All I can say is that until I reached men's competition, I never owned the shot. Power was enough to win. But then I learned that I had to vary my game, to keep adding new dimensions to my attack to stay on top. The drop shot fit perfectly in that plan.

The drop shot can lift your game, too, provided you practice it and use it wisely.

KEYS TO THE DROP SHOT

DISGUISE YOUR BACKSWING

Your success with the drop shot hinges on how well you can disguise it. If you tip your hand, your opponent will probably be able to reach the ball and make a return.

To hide your intentions of hitting a drop shot, start your racquet back the same way you would to hit a slice ground stroke, as I'm demonstrating in photo 1 below. I think my ability to disguise the shot is especially effective because my backswing for every stroke is compact. From this position, I can either drive the ball deep or drop it over the net.

Your forward stroke should be smooth, from high to low (2 and 3). Starting with my racquet at about shoulder level, I swing smoothly forward and downward at an angle.

3

TAKE THE PACE OFF THE BALL

With a relaxed grip, I take a lot of pace off my opponent's return (4). Notice that I open my racquet face slightly at contact to help put backspin on the ball and hit it on a gentle arc to clear the net.

Here's where a lot of club players make their mistakes on the drop shot. Instead of hitting through the ball, they stop their racquets quickly after the ball has been hit. This jerky motion tends to pop the ball too deep.

The follow-through for the drop shot isn't as long as one for a ground stroke, but it's just as important for control. You can see in photos 5 through 7 that my racquet head continues to move forward smoothly after contact has been made in a short follow-through.

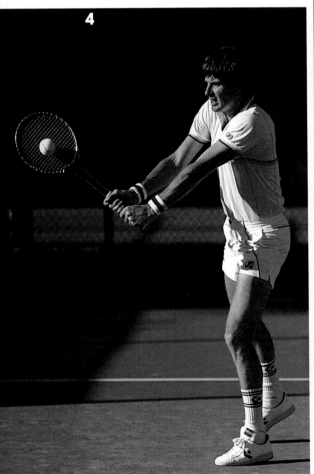

THE ANGLED PASSING SHOT:
USE THIS RISKY WEAPON WISELY

There's no doubt about it. Tennis is a game of distractions. Every time you step out on court to play, you're surrounded by them.

First, there are the distractions of the court environment. Each year at the U.S. Open in Flushing Meadow, N.Y., for example, players have to cope not only with nature's distractions like the sun, heat and wind, but also with airplane and train noise, restless crowds and all the pluses and minuses of life in the big city. I've learned to thrive on those distractions, but they drive some players crazy.

And then, of course, there are the distractions of play—the tactics, the shot selection, even the gamesmanship—that can occur on court during a match.

The player who's able to take all these distractions in stride and, in turn, give his opponent a few more to handle is going to be a winner. That applies to club players as well as to the pros.

One way to distract an opponent's concentration on court without going the gamesmanship route, is to attempt an unexpected shot. Your surprise tactic might start him thinking about what you'll do next in a similar situation. And we all know that thinking too much on court is more likely to hurt a player's game than help it.

One of the shots I'll occasionally use—and I emphasize the word occasionally—to try to throw a wrench into my opponent's concentration is an off-speed, sharply angled passing shot. It's a tough shot to hit and it's extremely risky, but it can pay off in the right situation.

I'm most likely to hit the sharply angled pass off a weak approach shot to my backhand side. There are two reasons for that preference. First, my two-handed grip gives me a little more control than I have with my forehand. Second, my opponent's weak approach shot allows me to step into the court and meet the ball way out in front of my body, a key factor in the stroke.

What makes the shot successful is that I'll usually catch my opponents totally by surprise with it. Sometimes, I'll even surprise myself with the decision to try it. Seriously, though, my opponents through the years have become accustomed to my powerful passing shots. Those are the strokes

A low-percentage shot: The sharply angled pass (left) is an advanced stroke, one that requires great timing and touch.

One way to distract an opponent's concentration on court is to attempt an unexpected shot.

Early contact: In order to pull the ball sharply, I have to meet the ball farther out in front of my body (right) than I would for a normal crosscourt ground stroke.

that have brought me my success in the game. They've been my bread and butter.

So when I catch the ball perfectly on an angled passing shot attempt, the relatively slow speed and placement near the singles sideline will force my net-rushing opponent to lunge sideways for the ball. The chances are that he'll reach it, but his return will probably be weak. I make sure I'm there waiting for the ball if it comes back over the net.

Again, I must stress that I'll only attempt this shot on rare occasions. Nine times out of 10, I'll hit a solid passing shot. An offensive lob is my second-best choice and the sharply angled pass is a distant third on my list of priorities. In fact, I may hit only one of these shots every three matches or so.

For that reason, I don't recommend the shot for an intermediate-level club player. The sharply angled pass is an advanced stroke. Even if you have a lot of talent, you should try it only when you find yourself well ahead in a game and you feel you can afford to lose the point.

The shot calls for great timing and touch. Your first goal in the stroke is to take the ball quickly after it bounces so that it doesn't get up too high. In my mind, I'm always thinking I have to play the ball aggressively and not let the ball play me. If I let it rise too high and deep before I make contact, there's absolutely no chance I can hit the shot with the control that's required.

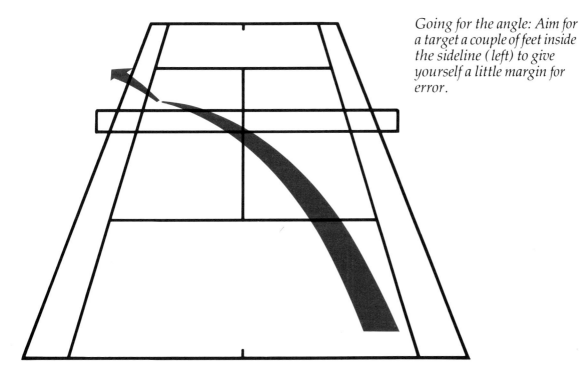

Going for the angle: Aim for a target a couple of feet inside the sideline (left) to give yourself a little margin for error.

The swing itself is a short one. I use the same backswing as I do on my regular ground strokes, and that convinces my opponent that he's got to get ready for a driving passing shot, my specialty. But from there, the stroke changes drastically.

Instead of powering the racquet head through the contact zone and finishing in a complete follow-through, I'll slow down the swing and cut it short. I keep a tight grip on the racquet and just roll the ball crosscourt with moderate pace.

You've probably seen other pros use the sharply angled passing shot a lot more often than I do. Bjorn Borg, Ivan Lendl, John McEnroe and Ilie Nastase are just a few who have made it a legitimate weapon in their attacks. But each of them hits the shot differently than I do, relying more on spin.

Borg and Lendl, for example, blast the ball with topspin, which helps bring the ball down in the court within the sideline very quickly. McEnroe and Nastase use more underspin than topspin to plop the ball over the net, but they've had success with the shot as well. I suggest that you use a moderate amount of topspin, at least at first, to reduce your chances of mistiming the hit.

Finally, remember to close in on the net after you hit the angled cross-court pass. Your chances of hitting an outright winner are slim unless you stroke the ball perfectly. I always count on my opponent reaching the ball even though he may have to dive for it because I don't go for the line with the shot.

My philosophy is I'd rather give him the chance to return the ball by placing the shot a little inside the sideline. The chances are his shot will be weak and that will give me a better opportunity to pass him cleanly with my next shot, most likely a crosscourt volley.

So if you're feeling adventuresome, if everything you're hitting in a match is working perfectly, then you might consider giving the sharply angled passing shot a try. Even if your attempt goes wide, you'll probably give your opponent second thoughts about what you'll try next. It could pay off in the form of a few important points.

KEYS TO THE ANGLED PASSING SHOT

GET INTO A BALANCED HITTING POSITION

The sharply angled crosscourt pass is one of the riskiest shots in the game. There isn't much margin for error in terms of the amount of court you have to work with.

Timing, therefore, becomes critical. My first move on the return is to move into a balanced hitting stance with good footwork (see photos 1 and 2).

Notice that my backswing at this point (3) doesn't give away my intention to hit the off-speed shot. As far as my opponent can tell, I'm about to fire the type of powerful passing shot that's become a trademark of my game. You should try to disguise the shot as well.

3

4

5

BRUSH UP ON THE BALL TO ROLL IT CROSSCOURT

Unlike Borg or Lendl who both use heavy topspin on the shot, I swing toward the ball with a flatter, more direct stroke (4). Keeping a firm grip on the racquet, I make contact with the ball farther out in front of my body (5) than I would on a normal crosscourt ground stroke because I have to pull the ball more sharply toward the sideline.

Then, I gently roll the ball crosscourt with an upward brushing motion (6), aiming for a target area about midway back in my opponent's service box and near the singles sideline.

The follow-through on the sharp-angled pass is shorter and more vertical than on a normal ground stroke (7). It indicates that I've taken some speed off the ball and made a smooth stroke.

THE SKYHOOK:
PICK OFF OFFENSIVE LOBS IN THE AIR

Over the years, I'd say the skyhook has become my most famous shot because it's a unique, dramatic stroke that the fans enjoy seeing. But make no mistake, I don't use the stiff-arm type of overhead just for show.

I use the skyhook because it gets the job done for me. When I hit it, I'm often able to turn the tables on an opponent who's hit what looks to be a good offensive lob and instead, put him on the defensive.

In fact, the skyhook has been working for me for a long, long time, even back in my younger days. As a kid, I wasn't very tall or strong so I didn't have much of an overhead. I just stiff-armed a lot of deep floaters and refined the shot enough to make it a valuable weapon. It's still an important shot in my game—especially these days, because I'm going to the net more often than I have in the past. That gives my opponents a few more opportunities to lob over me.

The mechanics of my skyhook are actually quite simple, but it's not the type of shot you see club pros trying to teach their students. It's a stroke that requires a lot of coordination and excellent timing to pull off consistently. It's got to be an instinctive shot.

As soon as the ball leaves my opponent's racquet, I know whether I'll be able to hit a regular overhead or have to rely on the skyhook. If I have the chance, of course, I'll go for the simple overhead because I can hit it with more power and control.

But if the ball is too deep, especially over my backhand side, I'll automatically prepare for the skyhook. The name of the game at this point of the stroking exchange is just to get my body into good enough position to reach the ball. As you can see in the photo sequence that follows, I take a quick step or two backward to put me within range.

Meanwhile, I'm extending my racquet out behind me and below the level of my rear knee. I jump off my back foot in a scissors kick and begin my upward stroke. I call it a windmill-type swing because my arm and racquet are kept straight and stiff right through contact with the ball.

This windmill action is important. First, it gives me maximum reach. →

All-out effort: The skyhook (left) is a crowd-pleaser because it's a dramatic stroke that stretches me to my limits.

The skyhook is a stroke that requires a lot of coordination and excellent timing to pull off consistently.

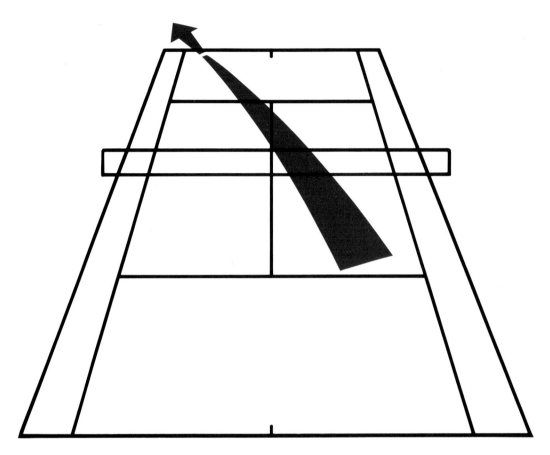

Turning the tables: If I'm able to make good contact on my skyhook, I'll send the ball deep (above). With a little luck, it will surprise my opponent.

Second, it gives the racquet head a lot more momentum than if I had started my stroke from behind my back as I would on a regular overhead. And because I'm falling backward at contact and my shoulders are facing the net, that momentum, along with a strong wrist snap through contact, translates into a more powerful shot.

The trickiest part of the skyhook is meeting the ball solidly. That's because I can't see the ball at contact. My racquet actually meets the ball well behind my head and there's no way I can turn around to see it and still keep my balance. There's a certain amount of instinct or educated guesswork needed to know where the ball is when you can't see it.

There really isn't much of a follow-through on the skyhook. I'm more concerned with landing on the court on my feet, not my derriere, to worry much about where my racquet should be. I just concentrate on letting the racquet head move smoothly through impact and not slowing it down.

I've been told a number of times by people in the stands that it looks like it takes a great amount of effort to hit the skyhook. Maybe that's why it's such a crowd-pleaser. It *is* a tough shot, but I'll tell you one thing: The skyhook saves me a lot of work trying to chase down offensive lobs that are bouncing away from me!

KEYS TO THE SKYHOOK

REACT QUICKLY BY STEPPING BACK

The skyhook is a very demanding stroke that requires quick reflexes. Because your opponent's offensive lob won't be in the air as long as a defensive lob, you have to retreat purposefully.

As soon as I see that an offensive lob might be within reach, I turn and step back (photos 1 and 2 below) and extend my arm and racquet low behind me, at about knee level.

USE A STIFF-ARM SWING TO MAKE CONTACT

Once I know I'm within range, I carefully time a jump off my back foot (3 and 4) and start my racquet up with a stiff-arm, windmill type of swing (5). This motion gives me maximum upward reach and my racquet extra momentum.

Making good contact with the ball is strictly a matter of timing and experience because impact usually occurs behind my head and out of sight (6).

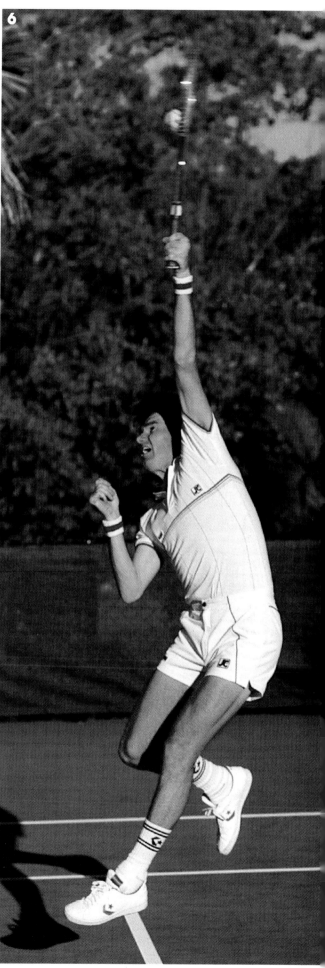

7

BRACE YOURSELF FOR A ROUGH LANDING

The follow-through for the skyhook is a natural one. There's simply no way you can hit the ball with the motion I've just described without your arm and racquet naturally continuing out in front of you (7).

In fact, I've never had to think about or check my follow-through because I'm always more concerned with making a landing. It's often a rough one, but if you maintain your balance (8 and 9), you're probably in good shape to regain an attacking position at the net.

HOW TO
GET THE MOST OUT OF
PRACTICE SESSIONS

Whenever I'm warming up for a match, regardless of whether I'm at the U.S. Open, Wimbledon or any of the smaller Grand Prix events, I firmly believe that by the time the final shot has been hit in the contest, I'll be the one walking away as the winner. To some, that may sound like cockiness. I think it's the result of having confidence in my game.

There's no doubt in my mind that if your goal is to become a tough, consistent competitor, that's the type of attitude you need to develop. Of course, social tennis doesn't require the same level of confidence. But still, I think you'll have to admit that even in matches for fun, it's nice to finish on top.

I'm not talking about going into a match simply telling yourself, convincing yourself, that you'll win. If you do that, all you're building is a phony confidence. Your opponent will probably shoot it down quicker than he can pick off a short defensive lob. So that approach leads down a dead-end road to a lot of frustration.

What you should be after is the real thing. And there's only one way to build that kind of confidence to a level where you feel great going into pre-match warm-ups. That is to practice often enough and long enough to suit your game, your talents and your personality. Deep down inside of you, you've got to know what you're capable of doing on court and what your limitations are as well.

I'm not writing a blank prescription for you to practice for hours on end each day. Every player's practice needs vary. For example, you might benefit, and even enjoy, such a tough training regimen. Your next door neighbor, on the other hand, may practice only a third as much as you, but

Tournament workouts: On the day of a match, I'll play a practice set or two (right) with another player, then quit.

see just as much improvement in his game.

That's why a lot of kids today don't get much out of the intense tennis training academies that are found scattered across the country today. If they're not the type of players who need to be drilled and drilled on court in strict practice routines, they often lose interest in the game. It's not fun anymore. As a result, they might turn to another sport or activity before they ever reach their full potential on the tennis court.

I'm one of the players who doesn't enjoy regular, structured practices. I've never been one to go out every day and hit crosscourt forehands for 10 minutes, crosscourt backhands for another 10 and so on through all the strokes. I would much rather go out, hit a few balls to loosen up and then say to my practice partner, "Serve them up. Let's play!"

Of course, my situation isn't the norm. Throughout my career, I've reached the late rounds of most of the events I've entered. That translates into a lot of play during a tournament week. So if I practiced for a few hours each day during tournaments, I'd probably leave my game on the practice court. I'd be worn out by the time the actual match started.

On the day of a match, I'll go out in the morning and practice for about 40 minutes. That's all. I'll play a practice set or two with another player and then quit. Next, I'll go back to my hotel, have lunch and relax. I won't go back to the tournament site until about an hour before my match so that I can keep my mind off the game. The one-hour cushion of time allows me to prepare for the match at my own pace, so that I don't feel rushed.

During weeks when I'm off, I'll usually play sets for a couple of hours a day. If I can't find another touring pro to practice with, that's when I'll try to hit with a teaching pro. For example, when I lived in North Miami Beach, Fla., I'd occasionally work out with Fred Stolle, the former Australian tennis star.

In order to make the most of the time he had to offer, I would do all of the moving in our sessions while he fed the ball accurately. A typical workout might go something like this. First, I'd have to play every shot into one corner. Fred would stand in the deuce corner and I'd have to hit every one of my shots to that side. After about 10 minutes, he'd move over to the ad side. That would become my new target area.

Finally, he would come to the net and I'd hit passing shots to each side. All of this time, he'd be moving me around the court. About 40 minutes into the workout, I'd serve a few balls to catch my breath. Then, I'd repeat the whole routine.

By the time I finished the second round, my legs felt dead. Any extra time I practiced beyond this point, I considered a double-time bonus. In other words, playing another 15 minutes was just like playing another half hour. Obviously, that kind of workout was intense and exhausting. And it helped provide a change of pace for me on off weeks, but it was totally impractical during a tournament.

*Structured sessions: On off-weeks, I'll occasion-
ally enlist the help of a good pro like Fred
Stolle (above right) to give me a good workout.*

Such a routine might be impractical for your lifestyle. Let's say you've
got a court for the season and you've spent a hard day at the office or at
home. Probably the last thing you want to do is use your court time for
practice drills. You want to get out on court and run, play and socialize a
little, clear your mind of all the problems and details you've had to deal
with earlier in the day.

I understand the way you feel. Tennis is excellent therapy. Whenever I
step on the court and begin playing, all of my problems and concerns tend
to fade away as well. However, you should realize that there is a way to

There is no magic practice formula. You should tailor a personal practice plan to suit your game and personality.

incorporate some practice into your playing time without resorting to structured drills.

How? By picking out a weak link of your game and working on it as you play. For example, if you've always played a baseline game but would like to become more aggressive, a social match situation is the perfect chance for you to experiment with advancing to the net behind your approach shots or serves. Similarly, if you've watched your ground strokes fall shorter and shorter into your opponent's court in recent weeks, you might try to concentrate on hitting the ball with good depth.

In short, set a specific objective for yourself before you walk on court. There's not much pressure on you to win and the added challenge is likely to make the game even more exciting. I'm certain you'll also raise the level of your play simply by working toward a goal.

The same advice holds true if you take the game more seriously and you have the time to devote to regular practice sessions. You should practice with a purpose. Personally, it would really frustrate me to practice for three or four hours in the morning, walk away and two hours later say to myself, "Gee, I wish I had worked a little harder on this or that." It's the quality of the time you spend practicing that counts, not the length of time.

One way to help make sure that you follow through on that principle is to find a practice partner who is as eager as you are to improve his tennis, someone who doesn't mind standing there and feeding you balls for 15 to 20 minutes at a time, as long as you return the favor. Remember that practice is a two-way street. Don't monopolize your practice sessions or you won't keep your partners for long.

Another option is to enlist the services of a teaching pro who takes an active interest in his students. It helps to have someone monitor your workouts, especially when you're younger, because that way you're less likely to waste time. My mom always supervised my practices when I was a junior. If I worked hard in a solid session of about 45 minutes, she'd come over and say something like, "O.K., that's enough. Why don't you go and ride your horse or play with your brother."

At that point, I would feel great because it meant two things. First, I had a good day on court and worked hard on my game. And second, I could take off and do whatever else I wanted.

It's pretty rare for a player to know himself so well that he can work effectively on his own in practice. So if you're serious about improving, find a pro who knows your limits and your goals in the game. You'll see the payoff almost immediately on court.

There is no magic practice formula that will work for every tennis player, of course. I wish I could give you one. What's most important is that you tailor your own practice plan around your game and your personality. Once you find what works best, you should be able to warm up more confidently for your matches with a winner's attitude.

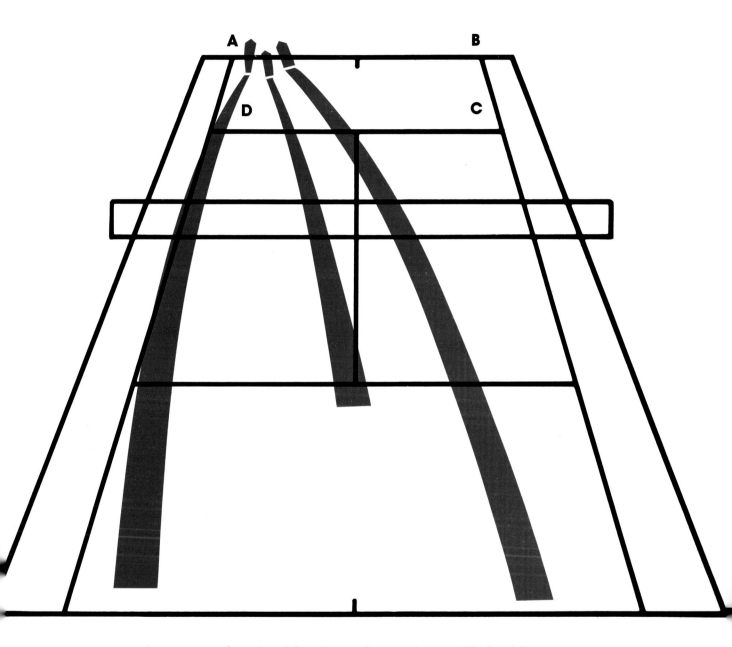

A concentrated routine: When I can't play practice sets, I'll often follow a structured routine like the one above. I start by placing all of my shots to the deuce corner (A above) for about 10 minutes, and then to the ad corner (B). Next, my practice partner will come to the net and I'll have to hit passing shots to each side (C and D) for another 10 minutes.

After serving a few balls to catch my breath, I'll repeat the drills. At the end of an hour and a half, I'm always soaked to the bone and exhausted, but the session helps sharpen my game.

SURE-FIRE WAYS TO SIZE UP AN UNKNOWN OPPONENT

A s much as I benefit from tennis in the material sense, nothing can compare with the enjoyment I get out of facing the constant challenges it presents. Every time I step on the court for a match, I face a new set of variables—the playing conditions, the sharpness of my game, the way my opponent is playing.

After all these years, tennis is, first and foremost, still a game for me in the true sense of the word. So every new challenge that comes along helps to make the game more interesting.

Unfamiliar opponents fall into that category. They are usually young players who've quickly come up through the junior or qualifying ranks and are thirsty for their first major win. My challenge is to make sure their big break doesn't come at my expense.

That's a goal that any player, amateur or pro, should set for himself. And it can be a tough one to live up to, especially if you're a good player, because the young kids today are more aggressive and fearless than ever and feel they have little to lose.

I used to be one of those juniors. In fact, my first big win came over the great Australian serve-and-volleyer Roy Emerson, at Los Angeles in 1969. I remember I went into that match a relative unknown and when I left as the winner, I learned I had been awarded a locker in the same room with the big boys. It was a great thrill.

Freewheeling juniors, of course, aren't the only unfamiliar players you're likely to come up against at the club level. I've been around the game so long, it's pretty rare for me to lock horns with someone I've never seen play before or at least heard about. But you're in a different boat. You're more likely to run into a wider variety of opponents and there may not be any information on them in your club's grapevine.

Whether you're a proven champ or an intermediate player who simply enjoys playing social tennis, how can you more consistently conquer the unknown competitor across the net? Here's some advice that I think may prove helpful.

Before the match, you first must make an important mental adjustment. If you're a top player, your record may be well known to your opponent. That can work to your advantage, of course, if it makes him a bit tentative

An early assessment: You'd be surprised how much you can learn about a player in the warm-up if you train yourself to be observant (left).

I'm very wary of unfamiliar players. That keeps me prepared for anything.

with his shots. In that type of a situation, for example, I'll often be able to jump out to a quick start so that by the time my opponent pulls himself together, I'm on a roll that's tough to stop.

On the other hand, I've learned you can never count on that happening. More than a few times in my career, I've squared off against young players who are loose and really rip the ball at the start of play. After a few tough games, though, I'll usually find my rhythm, forcing them to stumble a little. Suddenly, when they find they're not hitting the winners they were at first, they'll often try to go for too much with their shots and fall into a trap they can't escape. Still, I'm wary of unfamiliar players. That cautious attitude keeps me prepared for anything once the first ball is put into play.

If you are just an average player, a good mental attitude is perhaps even more crucial to your success against an unfamiliar player. Why? Because you have to remember that he probably doesn't know anything more about your game than you know about his. In other words, you're both on even terms going into your match. The player who can put aside his fears of the unknown is the one who is most likely to take control of the battle at the outset.

Once you're on court for the warm-up, you have to size him up quickly in terms of stroking skills. That's a job many club players tend to overlook. I'm talking about watching an opponent's general hitting style and getting a feel for his strengths and weaknesses during the pre–match warm-up period and the opening few games of the first set.

What about scouting an opponent during one of his previous matches? If you're dead set on winning a match, I suppose it's an effective means of getting an edge on someone. But personally, I've never believed in scouting an opponent because it would lessen the challenge for me on court.

In social tennis, I really don't think there's a place for it, either. At that level, you should go on court to have fun, not blow away your opponent 6-0, 6-0.

The warm-up is where evaluating an opponent's game first begins. You only have five minutes or so to work with, but you'd be surprised how much you can learn if you train yourself to be observant.

I'm not necessarily talking about looking for small details, such as your opponent's grips, which could give you some clues about how you should attack. I know many of the pros do that, but I try to evaluate my opponents in more general terms.

What I like to do against an unfamiliar opponent is watch his stroking style. I make mental notes about the type of spin he likes to use, the size of his swing (a player with a huge, roundhouse swing may be prone to mistime his hits) and any obvious nervousness. These little observations can come in handy during play.

There are two major things the warm-up cannot reveal about a player. The first is the efficiency of his footwork (how fast he's able to reach the ball) because he's not running all-out during the warm-up. Second, you can never tell how well he competes under pressure because there hasn't been any yet. You may not find your answer until he's a break point down at 5-all in the second set.

Obviously, the first few games of your match will fill any gaps you might have missed in the warm-up. I like to compare this stage of the match with a boxing bout. Smart boxers won't enter the ring against an unknown fighter and start throwing their best punches when the bell rings for the first round. In the same way, I don't want to go out and throw my best stuff at an opponent unless I see that he's so nervous he's ready to crack right at the outset.

So what I'll often do is fire a few jabs and move the ball around a little bit to get a feel for how he plays. If I've spotted an obvious weakness in his game, I might not go after it right away. Sometimes, I'll hit to his strength and try to break it down. If I'm able to do that, the rest of the match is usually history. But even if I can't, I still have that weakness I discovered in the warm-up to fall back on. I recommend that you try the same strategy.

Occasionally, this initial feeling-out process will appear to work against you. In other words, your opponent may jump out to a quick lead if he's loose and confident. It's happened to me. In that situation, you have to hang tough and reject any tendency to panic. When your game finally kicks into gear, you should be able to apply the brakes and halt your opponent, using the mental notes you made earlier in the match.

My final advice for playing an unfamiliar opponent is this: Go out and play your own game. Try to put yourself in control of the situation when you first step on the court. Get a good feel for the environment and the match circumstances.

Most of all, don't feel that you have to become highly technical in picking out a weakness. Keep your early assessment of his game simple . . . and capitalize on that knowledge. It's worked for me and it can work for you, too.

HUSTLE
FOR MORE FUN &
SUCCESS ON COURT

In any sport, they say you can't hope to be considered a great champion until you've proved that you can win regularly, even when you're not playing at top form. The champion finds ways to pull himself through tough situations; he doesn't buckle under pressure, and he doesn't quit trying.

Those last four words are the key to the whole thought: He doesn't quit trying. Whether you're a club champion, a ranked junior, a social player, a weekend hacker or beginner, you should live by those words on the tennis court because they'll help you get more enjoyment and satisfaction out of playing the game and help you realize your full potential at whatever level of play you choose.

I pride myself on being able to say that throughout my career, I've always walked off the court following a match knowing that I gave a 100 percent effort. Of course, that type of total effort doesn't guarantee a win. What it does guarantee, however, is that I do my best in each and every match.

I hustle for shots, I get into the flow of play, I don't allow pressure situations to overcome me. When I do lose, I at least have the satisfaction of knowing that my opponent beat me. I didn't hand him the match because I didn't try. For me, that would be the ultimate rip-off. I'd be cheating myself and the fans. I'd give up the game totally if I ever reached that level of frustration.

More often than not, putting out 100 percent efforts on court has produced some important victories for me. Of course, the days when you blow away opponents, when everything in your game seems to click perfectly, are great. But the days when your timing or concentration are a bit off are when total efforts really pay off. →

A total effort: By hustling on every point (right) I've found I can wear down opponents and overcome pressure situations.

Never, never quit until the last ball has been played.

For example, I faced that type of situation in the quarterfinals of the 1978 U.S. Open. Going into the event, I felt I was playing good enough tennis to win the title. Beyond that, the Open's move to hard courts at Flushing Meadow, N.Y., gave me additional incentive. I was as determined as ever to win at the new site, in front of the New York fans.

But Italy's Adriano Panatta—a talented player who hit fantastic, although occasionally erratic shots—gave me a real scare in the quarters. After splitting the first four sets, he broke me early in the fifth and served for the match at 5-4.

After three and a half hours of tough play, I had to kick myself and my game into gear or be eliminated. Fortunately, I was able to meet the challenge with a couple of tough service returns that nailed down a service break. I was really pumped up with adrenaline.

Panatta's last service game at 5-6 was a 15-minute marathon. Down 0-40, he saved three match points, but I finally earned an ad point by firing an all-or-nothing, one-handed backhand passing shot down the line from wide of the court that caught him by surprise. It shook him, and he double-faulted on the next point to end the match.

By hustling on every point, I was able to rise to the occasion when it mattered most in that match. The lesson to be learned here is: Never, never quit until the last ball has been played.

That simple philosophy can work wonders for your game, regardless of your playing ability. At a highly competitive level, for example, you'll be able to win more long matches. Your opponents will soon learn that you're a fighter, that you'll never give in or crack under pressure. As a result, they'll know they're the ones who are under fire in the late stages of a match. It won't be easy for them to put the finishing touches on a win.

At a more recreational or social level, your new hang-tough attitude will help make the game more exciting. After a long day at work, home or school, you'll look forward to getting out on the court and enjoying some healthy exercise that will take your mind off your everyday problems.

You'll also realize two other important benefits of putting out 100 percent efforts on court. First, your game will improve more quickly than you ever thought possible. And second, you'll have more fun than ever before.

So go ahead and enjoy yourself. Serve them up!

The final handshake: Whether you've won or lost, a 100 percent effort should leave you with a sense of inner satisfaction.

JIMMY CONNORS'
CAREER CHAMPIONSHIPS

1972

1.	Jan.	16	Jacksonville (Fla.) International	d. Clark Graebner
2.	Jan.	23	Roanoke (Va.) International	d. Vladimir Zednick
3.	June	24	Queens, England	d. John Paish
4.	July	23	Columbus, Ohio	d. Andrew Pattison
5.	Aug.	6	Cincinnati, Ohio	d. Guillermo Vilas
6.	Oct.	1	Albany, N.Y.	d. Roscoe Tanner

1973

7.	Jan.	7	Baltimore (Md.) Indoors	d. Sandy Mayer
8.	Jan.	21	Roanoke (VA.) International	d. Ian Fletcher
9.	Feb.	11	Salt Lake City, Utah	d. Paul Gerken
10.	Feb.	24	Salisbury, Md.	d. Karl Meiler
11.	March	3	Hampton (Va.) International	d. Ilie Nastase
12.	March	10	Paramus (N.J.) International	d. Clark Graebner
13.	July	23	U.S. Pro, Boston, Mass.	d. Arthur Ashe
14.	Aug.	5	Columbus, Ohio	d. Charlie Pasarell
15.	Sept.	23	Los Angeles, Calif.	d. Tom Okker
16.	Oct.	7	Quebec, Canada	d. Marty Riessen
17.	Nov.	27	Johannesburg, S. Africa	d. Arthur Ashe

1974

18.	Jan.	1	Australian Chps., Melbourne	d. Phil Dent
19.	Jan.	20	Roanoke (Va.) International	d. Karl Meiler
20.	Feb.	10	Little Rock, Ark.	d. Karl Meiler
21.	Feb.	14	Birmingham (Ala.) International	d. Sandy Mayer
22.	Feb.	24	Salisbury, Md.	d. Frew McMillan
23.	March	10	Hampton (Va.) International	d. Ilie Nastase
24.	March	24	Salt Lake City, Utah	d. Vitas Gerulaitis
25.	March	31	Tempe, Ariz.	d. Vijay Amritraj
26.	June	8	Manchester, England	d. Michael Collins
27.	July	7	Wimbledon, England	d. Ken Rosewall
28.	Aug.	11	U.S. Clay, Indianapolis, Ind.	d. Bjorn Borg
29.	Sept.	8	U.S. Open, Forest Hills, N.Y.	d. Ken Rosewall
30.	Sept.	22	Los Angeles, Calif.	d. Harold Solomon
31.	Nov.	16	London, England	d. Brian Gottfried
32.	Nov.	26	Johannesburg, S. Africa	d. Arthur Ashe

1975

33.	Jan.	18	Freeport International, Bahamas	d. Karl Meiler
34.	Feb.	16	Salisbury, Md.	d. Vitas Gerulaitis
35.	Feb.	23	Boca Raton, Fla.	d. Jurgen Fassbender
36.	March	16	Hampton (Va.) International	d. Jan Kodes
37.	April	20	Denver, Colo.	d. Brian Gottfried
38.	June	26	Birmingham (Ala.) International	d. Billy Martin
39.	Aug.	9	North Conway, N.H.	d. Ken Rosewall
40.	Sept.	21	Princess Classic, Bermuda	d. Vitas Gerulaitis
41.	Oct.	5	Maui, Hawaii	d. Sandy Mayer

1976

42.	Jan.	25	Birmingham (Ala.) International	d. Roscoe Tanner
43.	Feb.	1	U.S. Pro Indoor, Philadelphia, Pa.	d. Bjorn Borg
44.	March	14	Hampton (Va.) International	d. Ilie Nastase
45.	March	28	Palm Springs, Calif.	d. Roscoe Tanner
46.	April	25	Denver, Colo.	d. Ross Case
47.	May	16	Las Vegas, Nev.	d. Ken Rosewall
48.	July	26	Washington, D.C.	d. Raul Ramirez
49.	Aug.	8	North Conway, N.H.	d. Raul Ramirez
50.	Aug.	16	U.S. Clay, Indianapolis, Ind.	d. Wojtek Fibak
51.	Sept.	12	U.S. Open, Forest Hills, N.Y.	d. Bjorn Borg
52.	Nov.	7	Cologne, France	d. Frew McMillan
53.	Nov.	21	Wembley, England	d. Roscoe Tanner

1977	54. Jan.	8	Masters, N.Y.	d.	Bjorn Borg
	55. Jan.	16	Birmingham (Ala.) International	d.	Bill Scanlon
	56. March	20	St. Louis, Mo.	d.	John Alexander
	57. May	1	Las Vegas, Nev.	d.	Raul Ramirez
	58. May	15	WCT Finals, Dallas, Tex.	d.	Dick Stockton
	59. Oct.	9	Maui, Hawaii	d.	Brian Gottfried
	60. Oct.	23	Sydney, Australia	d.	Brian Gottfried
1978	61. Jan.	29	U.S. Pro Indoor, Phila., Pa.	d.	Roscoe Tanner
	62. Feb.	26	Denver, Colo.	d.	Stan Smith
	63. March	5	Memphis, Tenn.	d.	Tim Gullikson
	64. April	9	Rotterdam, Netherlands	d.	Raul Ramirez
	65. June	18	Birmingham, England	d.	Raul Ramirez
	66. July	23	Washington, D.C.	d.	Eddie Dibbs
	67. Aug.	13	U.S. Clay, Indianapolis, Ind.	d.	Jose Higueras
	68. Aug.	20	Stowe, Vt.	d.	Tim Gullikson
	69. Sept.	10	U.S. Open, Flushing Mead., N.Y.	d.	Bjorn Borg
	70. Oct.	22	Sydney, Australia	d.	Geoff Masters
	71. Nov.	20	WCT Challenge, Las Vegas, Nev.	d.	Roscoe Tanner
1979	72. Jan.	21	Birmingham (Ala.) International	d.	Eddie Dibbs
	73. Jan.	28	U.S. Pro Indoor, Philadelphia, Pa.	d.	Arthur Ashe
	74. Feb.	25	WCT Chps., Dorado, Fla.	d.	Vitas Gerulaitis
	75. March	4	Memphis, Tenn.	d.	Arthur Ashe
	76. April	15	Tulsa, Okla.	d.	Eddie Dibbs
	77. Aug.	12	U.S. Clay, Indianapolis, Ind.	d.	Guillermo Vilas
	78. Aug.	19	Stowe, Vt.	d.	Mike Cahill
	79. Nov.	11	Hong Kong Classic	d.	Pat DuPre
1980	80. Jan.	20	Birmingham (Ala.) International	d.	Eliot Teltscher
	81. Jan.	27	U.S. Pro Indoor, Philadelphia, Pa.	d.	John McEnroe
	82. May	4	WCT Finals, Dallas, Tex.	d.	John McEnroe
	83. Aug.	3	North Conway, N.H.	d.	Eddie Dibbs
	84. Oct.	19	Canton, China	d.	Eliot Teltscher
	85. Nov.	2	Tokyo, Japan	d.	Tom Gullikson
1981	86. Feb.	22	La Quinta, Calif.	d.	Ivan Lendl
	87. March	15	Brussels, Belgium	d.	Brian Gottfried
	88. March	22	Rotterdam, Belgium	d.	Brian Gottfreid
	89. Nov.	15	London, England	d.	John McEnroe
1982	90. Feb.	28	Monterrey, Calif.	d.	Johan Kriek
	91. April	18	Los Angeles, Calif.	d.	Mel Purcell
	92. April	25	Las Vegas, Nev.	d.	Gene Mayer
	93. June	13	London, England	d.	John McEnroe
	94. July	4	Wimbledon, England	d.	John McEnroe
	95. Aug.	8	Columbus, Ohio	d.	Brian Gottfried
	96. Sept.	12	U.S. Open, Flushing Mead., N.Y.	d.	Ivan Lendl
1983	97. Feb.	14	Memphis, Tenn.	d.	Gene Mayer
	98. April	18	Las Vegas, Nev.	d.	Mark Edmondson
	99. June	6	London, England	d.	John McEnroe
	100. Sept.	11	U.S. Open, Flushing Mead., N.Y.	d.	Ivan Lendl
1984	101. Feb.	12	Memphis, Tenn.	d.	Henri Leconte
	102. Feb.	19	La Quinta, Calif.	d.	Yannick Noah
	103. April	1	Boca Raton, Fla.	d.	Johan Kriek
	104. Sept.	16	Los Angeles, Calif.	d.	Eliot Teltscher
	105. Oct.	21	Tokyo, Japan	d.	Ivan Lendl